Comments on other *Amazing Stories* from readers & reviewers

"Tightly written volumes filled with lots of wit and humour about famous and infamous Canadians."
Eric Shackleton, *The Globe and Mail*

"The heightened sense of drama and intrigue, combined with a good dose of human interest is what sets Amazing Stories *apart."*
Pamela Klaffke, *Calgary Herald*

"This is popular history as it should be... For this price, buy two and give one to a friend."
Terry Cook, a reader from Ottawa, on *Rebel Women*

"Glasner creates the moment of the explosion itself in graphic detail...she builds detail upon gruesome detail to create a convincingly authentic picture."
Peggy McKinnon, *The Sunday Herald*, on *The Halifax Explosion*

"It was wonderful...I found I could not put it down. I was sorry when it was completed."
Dorothy F. from Manitoba on *Marie-Anne Lagimodière*

"Stories are rich in description, and bristle with a clever, stylish realness."
Mark Weber, *Central Alberta Advisor*, on *Ghost Town Stories II*

"A compelling read. Bertin...has selected only the most intriguing tales, which she narrates with a wealth of detail."
Joyce Glasner, *New Brunswick Reader*, on *Strange Events*

"The resulting book is one readers will want to share with all the women in their lives."
Lynn Martel, *Rocky Mountain Outlook*, on *Women Explorers*

CHRISTMAS IN QUEBEC

CHRISTMAS IN QUEBEC

Heartwarming Legends,
Tales, and Traditions

HOLIDAY

by Megan Durnford

PUBLISHED BY ALTITUDE PUBLISHING CANADA LTD.
1500 Railway Avenue, Canmore, Alberta T1W 1P6
www.altitudepublishing.com
1-800-957-6888

Extreme care has been taken to ensure that all information presented in
this book is accurate and up to date. Neither the author nor the
publisher can be held responsible for any errors.

Publisher   Stephen Hutchings
Associate Publisher   Kara Turner
Series Editor   Jill Foran
Editor   Gayl Veinotte

We acknowledge the financial support of the Government
of Canada through the Book Publishing Industry Development
Program (BPIDP) for our publishing activities.

Altitude GreenTree Program
Altitude Publishing will plant twice as many trees as were used
in the manufacturing of this product.

We acknowledge the support of the Canada Council for the Arts which
in 2003 invested $21.7 million in writing and publishing throughout Canada.

Canada Council   Conseil des Arts
for the Arts   du Canada

National Library of Canada Cataloguing in Publication Data

Durnford, Megan
Christmas in Quebec / Megan Durnford.

(Amazing stories)
Includes bibliographical references.
ISBN 1-55153-784-2

1. Christmas--Quebec (Province) I. Title. II. Series: Amazing stories
(Canmore, Alta.)

GT4987.15.D87 2004   394.2663'09714   C2004-903751-X

An application for the trademark for Amazing Stories™
has been made and the registered trademark is pending.

Printed and bound in Canada by Friesens
2 4 6 8 9 7 5 3 1

To the loves of my life — Larry,
Charlotte, Hugh, and Philippe.
And to my father, Hugh Durnford, who instilled
in me a fascination for Canadian history.

Contents

Prologue

I was just returning from checking my traps when I saw a small plane circling above Bersimis. It was flying low — so low that it looked like it was going to land. I watched the plane and wondered who on earth would be bold enough to risk flying to our little settlement on the Côte-Nord in the wintertime. Today the weather was clear, but it wouldn't be for long. Terrible snowstorms had been plaguing the area for weeks, making almost any kind of travel impossible — even the best sled dogs were no match for the biting winds and blinding blizzards that were keeping the people of Bersimis at home. Though the holidays were fast approaching, the weather was making it difficult for any of us to get into the Christmas spirit.

I urged my sled dogs to slow down so I could watch the airplane more closely. Some of the other villagers had gathered to watch the plane as well. We looked at the sky and then at each other, trying to figure out what was going on. Why would a pilot dare make a trip so far north this time of year? And why was he just circling overhead?

Suddenly, a hefty grey bag came tumbling out of the plane and then the pilot flew away. Everyone was curious. We rushed towards the mysterious sack, all of us feeling like small children about to open stockings stuffed with gifts on Christmas morning. Samuel untied the rough cord and reached into the bag. Inside were letters and parcels for the villagers of Bersimis. Most of the letters had special Christmas stamps, and there was a great big package wrapped in red paper on which someone had scrawled "Joyeux Noël."

That pilot must have been Santa Claus himself...

Chapter 1
Les Fêtes: Quebec Holiday Traditions

I n Quebec, the Christmas holiday season is known as *Les Fêtes*. Today, there are many similarities between how Quebecers and other Canadians celebrate this season. However, for hundreds of years, up until the early part of the 20th century, *Les Fêtes* involved a unique set of religious and secular celebrations between Christmas Eve and Epiphany (January 6).

Christmas Eve

Christmas Eve in traditional French-Canadian society was synonymous with midnight mass. There were no stockings, presents, or Christmas trees on that holy night. Instead, December 24 was a solemn time, entirely focused on the celebration of Christ's birth.

The evening was one of the highlights of the year for early farming communities. In *Maria Chapdelaine*, a classic novel portraying 19th century Quebec, the heroine Maria is unable to attend midnight mass due to a snowstorm. She is absolutely devastated:

"As she watched the grey sky through a little window, she became sad. Going to midnight mass was the natural ambition and great desire of all French-Canadian families, even those who live far from the villages. All the obstacles they overcome — cold, nighttime in the woods, difficult roads and great distance — only add to the solemnity and the mystery of that night."

A Rural Christmas Scenario

In the 19th century, a typical family in Quebec would begin to prepare for Christmas weeks and weeks before the holiday arrived. The older children in the family spent countless hours rehearsing Christmas hymns for the midnight mass, Mother prepared special clothes for the sacred event, and all of the family members worked together to prepare festive dishes for the *réveillon*, or wake-up meal.

Around the first week of December, Father butchered a fattened pig, some chickens, and a sheep. Then, Mother and the aunts spent long days preparing sausages, ham, blood pudding, and meat pies. The women also prepared a host of sweets, such as doughnuts and dessert pies. The summer kitchen (a small room attached to the house but not heated

Habitants going to Christmas Market, 1842.

during the winter) was packed with delicacies.

By the time Christmas Eve finally arrived, the children could hardly contain their excitement. After devouring stacks of pancakes in the early evening, those who were over the age of 14 — and therefore entitled to go to midnight mass — took short naps. They knew that shortly after 10 p.m., while grandmother and the young ones slept on, they would be awakened and readied for the Christmas celebration.

After what seemed like only a few moments of slumber, the children rubbed their eyes and looked outside to see Father harnessing the horses and preparing the *cariole*, the family's sleigh. They donned their long red choir robes and scampered quietly downstairs, where Mother was setting the table for the *réveillon* meal.

Snow began to fall gently as the family clambered into

their *cariole*. With warm woolen clothing, bear skins on their laps, and hot bricks at their feet, they were hardly aware of the sub-zero temperature. Little bells on the horse's harness tinkled in response to the distant church bells, which were calling people to midnight mass. Sleighs began to arrive at the parish church, one after the other, for this special night of joy and mystery. The men hitched the horses to posts and then covered their animals with heavy blankets.

Hundreds of flickering candles cast a warm glow on the bundled-up villagers crowding into the church. Just before Christmas Eve, the *curé* (parish priest) had directed the community's young men to collect homemade tallow candles from all of the homes in the area. All the parishioners contributed generously to this Christmas ritual.

Suddenly, the best tenor soloist of the choir burst out triumphantly:

Minuit, Chrétiens,
C'est l'heure solonelle
Où l'homme Dieu descendit jusqu'à nous ...

Midnight mass had commenced.

All of the participants of the mass were resplendent in their ceremonial clothes. The sacristan (keeper of religious articles) wore a long, red, embroidered coat, and the choirboys were debonair in their long red or black robes. Churchwardens (lay assistants to the priests) wore long coats with pointed collars. The *curé* also wore his finest garments for this holy night.

The midnight mass was entirely sung in Latin by the cantor. Although not everyone in the congregation could follow the exact meaning of the liturgy, the exhilaration of the cantor's voice proclaiming Christ's birth was clear. After midnight mass, the *curé* celebrated the *messe de l'aurore* (mass of the dawn).

This mass was not quite as solemn as the midnight mass and the villagers were welcome to join the choir in singing traditional Christmas carols such as *Il est né le divin enfant, Les anges dans nos campagne, Ça berger, assemblons nous,* and *Nouvelle agréable.* Singing these cherished melodies helped everyone to stave off fatigue a little bit longer.

When the worship came to a close, each family went up to the *crèche* by the side altar to visit the infant Jesus lying in his manger. The villagers gazed at the babe with the rosy cheeks, lovingly swaddled in lace and linen. Then they left the church in a state of serene joy.

Outside in the crisp night air, friends and neighbours shouted Christmas greetings to each other as they got into their respective sleighs. Then it was time to rush home (around 2 a.m.) for the highly anticipated *réveillon.*

This meal was the first meal of *Les Fêtes* — a series of special family occasions between Christmas Eve and *Le Jour des Rois* (Epiphany). The *réveillon* itself was an intimate family meal, so no guests were invited.

After a long, sleigh ride in the wee hours of the morning,

Worshippers leaving midnight mass on Christmas Eve.

the family was very happy to be back in their cozy home. Thick logs of maple wood crackled in the fireplace, and the rooms were filled with the delicious smell of festive dishes, which had been simmering patiently.

The family roused grandmother and then they all sat down to a groaning board of homemade food, including *cretons* (a form of pâté), *ragoût* (meatballs and pig's feet in a rich gravy), *tourtière* (a mildly spiced meat pie), mashed potatoes, pickled vegetables, doughnuts, and *tarte au sucre* (maple syrup pie). Not surprisingly, the family slept late on Christmas morning.

New Year's Traditions

New Year's was a great celebration in traditional French-Canadian society. It was a time to make merry with friends and family and give presents to loved ones. It was also a time to feast!

La Guignolée

On December 31, French Canadians participated in a very important charity collection called *La Guignolée*. The most popular explanation for the origin of this term involves a New Year's ritual performed in ancient Gaul. Apparently, Celtic priests collected *feuilles du gui* (mistletoe) from sacred oak trees to herald the arrival of the New Year and then they exclaimed "*Au gui, l'an neuf.*" The inhabitants of New France brought this term with them from their homeland.

Guignolée collections began in Quebec in the early 1800s. On December 31, all the households in rural Quebec began to anticipate the arrival of the *guignoleux*, a group of villagers who collected food and money for underprivileged people in the community.

The ragtag troupe of *guignoleux* arrived at each doorstep by horse and sleigh. The large sleigh — ready to be filled as a horn of plenty — was usually gaily decorated with evergreen boughs, and sometimes torches were affixed to it.

The leader, in a heavy fur coat with a red sash, announced their arrival with a trumpet call. Then both the homeowner and the *guignoleux* engaged in a special ritual. While tapping

out the rhythm with long poles, the *guignoleux* began to sing
a song of supplication, which everyone knew by heart.

> *Bonjour le maitre et la maitresse*
> (Hello to the master and the mistress)
> *Et tous les gens de la maison*
> (And all of the people in the household)
> *Nous avons fait une promesse*
> (We have made a promise)
> *De venir vous voir une fois l'an*
> (To come visit you once a year)
> *Une fois l'an, ce n'est pas grand'chose*
> (Once a year is not a lot)
> *Qu'un petit morceau de chignée*
> (Just a little piece of pork)
> *Un petit morceau de chignée si vous voulez.*
> (A little piece of pork if you like.)

Naturally, there were dozens of variations of this song
across Quebec. Some versions gently teased the master and
mistress of the house, as in the following verse:

> *Si vous voulez rien nous donner*
> (If you don't want to give us anything)
> *Dites-nous lé*
> (Tell us)

Nous prendrons la fille ainée
(We will take the eldest girl)
*Nous y ferons chauffer les pieds entre la poêle et
la cheminée.*
(We will warm her feet between the stove and
the fireplace.)

Then, the master and mistress of the house would perform their role in the ritual by inviting the *guignoleux* into the house to warm up and to have a little drink of whisky or *rhum.* Sometimes a snack, such as a doughnut or a piece of bread, was offered as well. After drinking to their host's good health, the *guignoleux* would pick up the family's donations — which consisted of choice cuts of meat, potatoes and other root vegetables, preserves, and sometimes even firewood and clothing — and then set off with great fanfare to the next household, bellowing, "*Qui donne aux pauvres, prête a Dieu*" (Those who give to the poor, will be recognized by God). Every house in the parish was visited; sometimes that meant that the *guignoleux* were still going in the wee hours of the morning.

Unfortunately, there were some disgraceful abuses of this tradition, especially in the growing towns and cities of Quebec, where several groups of *guignoleux* did the rounds simultaneously. On some occasions, the food and/or money never made it to the poor people for whom it was intended. The 1857 *guignolée* in Montreal, however, was conducted with utmost honesty — a welcome surprise after years of unseemly behaviour. According to the *Dimanche-Matin* newspaper of January 2, 1857: "On the first night of the New Year, Montreal re-experienced a custom which we thought was gone. Groups of young men with drums and violin went out to collect the guignolée, they asked for money and a little food for the local poor ...we are happy to see that it did not cause any disorder, the guignoleux were content to laugh, sing and collect money for the underprivileged ... In the past there were many groups that became drunk, and got into fights with other groups. Also, too many young people forgot to give the fruits of their labour to the poor."

But then, three years later in 1860, there were so many incidents of drunk and rowdy *guignoleux* disturbing the peace (and sometimes even stealing the proceeds of the charity drive) that the mayor of Montreal decided to issue licences for the *guignolée* and policemen were ordered to supervise their activities.

Today, the term *guignolée* is still used in Quebec to describe charity collection during the holiday season. However, no colourful rituals are associated with the modern *guignolée*. It is simply another occasion to write a cheque for a charitable organization.

New Year's Day

New Year's Day was a time to visit with friends and family. In traditional French-Canadian society, the New Year started as soon as the children were able to wake up the patriarch of the family for the time-honoured New Year's blessing. Then the married children would arrive with their own families, and they, too, would ask for the father's blessing for the coming year. With all of his children and grandchildren gathered around him on bended knee waiting for the blessing, the father of the family was usually overcome with emotion. Naturally, most men responded with the words that their fathers had used before them. Some fathers simply made the sign of the cross with their hand and then uttered a simple phrase such as, "*Que le bon Dieu te bénisse comme je te bénis*" (May God give you his blessing as I have given you my blessing). Other fathers chose to list all of the family's blessings and wishes for the future and then end with, "Et le paradis a la fin de tes jours" (And paradise at the end of your days).

Once the blessing was bestowed it was gift time! Most children hung stockings at the end of their beds on December 31. When they woke up the next morning, they could usually count on receiving fruits, raisins, and candies such as barley sugar in animal forms. In some families, children also received practical gifts, such as clothing, on New Year's Day, as well as simple handmade toys, like wooden trucks and cloth dolls. The children did not necessarily think that Santa Claus had brought the gifts. Up until the mid-19th century, children were taught that the Infant Jesus had come during the night to deliver presents. Considering how influential the church was regarding every aspect of family life, children would have been easily convinced that it was the Baby Jesus bringing them gifts.

Then the family was off to the parish church for a special mass that included a New Year's blessing. This mass was as much a part of the day's celebrations as the gifts. Following church, the entire extended family gathered for a New Year's feast.

While the women of the family bustled around setting up tables and finishing the meal preparation, some of the men went out to offer New Year's wishes from their family to friends and neighbours and to catch up on the latest gossip. Naturally, it was *de rigueur* for the men to have a little drink at each home.

Serving New Year's dinner was a huge undertaking, as traditional French Canadian families had numerous children. It was not uncommon to seat 40 to 50 people! But it was yet another opportunity to enjoy the bounty of the family farm. Although this meal included many of the same dishes as the Christmas Eve *réveillon*, the New Year's meal was typically a grander meal, featuring a greater variety of dishes and a number of guests.

Most families enjoyed chicken and/or pork roasts (turkey was considered too expensive), *tourtière* and other meat pies, mashed potatoes, *boudin* (blood pudding), cooked vegetables, *ragoût*, and pickled vegetables. This would be followed by a vast array of desserts: *beignes* (doughnuts), *croquignoles* (slightly lighter dough than a *beigne* and prepared as round balls), *tarte au sucre*, and *tarte au ferlouche* (a molasses and raisin pie).

The main beverage during dinner was water, although the men sometimes started the meal with a glass of whiskey, and the women might have had a glass of homemade cherry or black currant wine.

After a washing-up marathon to clean hundreds of dishes, the family settled into other diversions, such as card games, storytelling, and candy making. While the children ran wildly through their grandparents' house, some family members would bring out a violin and some spoons for percussion. Time to dance!

As the towns and cities of Quebec grew, New Year's traditions continued in a similar fashion. Ritual social visits on New Year's Day were also a Scottish tradition. So in the city of Montreal, which had a significant population of Scottish immigrants, both Anglophones and Francophones were earnest visitors.

These social visits were a serious duty to strengthen bonds of friendship and to smooth over the disagreements of the previous year. Each family would set out their best wines and cakes, specially made for the occasion. Then the women of the household, dressed in their finest gowns, would wait in the drawing room for their visitors.

In the early 1800s, following an extended visit to Canada, Irish journalist Edward Allen Talbot wrote that

Christmas in Quebec

"New-Year's day is one of their [French-Canadians] most regularly observed holidays and is wholly devoted to feasting and salutations. On this day, every cottager, both in town and country, can boast of a table well laden with fine wines, rich sweetmeats and cakes of every description. It is the office of the gentleman to go from one house to another, for the purpose of reciprocating the compliments of the season, and partaking of the good cheer which is universally prepared."

In Montreal in the early 1800s, it was customary for small groups of men to spend most of New Year's Day visiting. They were entitled to stop at every house where any one of the men had even the most casual acquaintance. And, thanks to an old French custom, male visitors were allowed to kiss all the ladies of the house on New Year's Day. So it is not surprising that young, single men met with as many ladies as possible on that day.

Men who had numerous business and social acquaintances might have made as many as 80 social calls on New Year's Day. Considering that they would have been expected to have a little drink at each house, it is almost amazing that they found their way home again!

Epiphany

Le Jour des Rois, or Epiphany, marked the end of the holiday season known as *Les Fêtes*. According to biblical lore, Epiphany was when the three kings — Melchior, Caspar, and Balthazar — arrived in Bethlehem bearing gifts of gold, frankincense, and myrrh for the baby Jesus. In traditional French-Canadian society, most people attended a special mass on the *Jour des Rois.*

On the day before the mass, the sacristan of the parish church would have located the plaster representations of the three kings and their camels and placed them in the *crèche* (nativity scene), which the parishioners had been enjoying since midnight mass on December 24.

The *Jour des Rois* was also a very exciting occasion for children. After the church service, the family would return home for *gâteau des rois,* a special cake in which a bean was hidden. Whoever found the bean in his or her serving had to make a speech and was then crowned king or queen for the day. This tradition dates back to pre-Christian times, when ancient Greeks and Romans entertained themselves by electing a king of the feast.

Chapter 2
Holiday Folklore

Christmas has always been a special time of year. Even in contemporary society, people are more generous towards each other, children are on their best behaviour, and the poor and the sick among us regain a sense of hope — all because it is Christmastime!

In traditional French-Canadian society there were a number of wondrous and supernatural events associated with the celebration of Christmas. One common belief was that on Christmas night the dead could rise from their graves. According to old Quebec storytellers, the dead would leave their coffins and kneel together next to a cross in the cemetery. Then a priest in a white surplice with a golden stole would arrive and recite the prayers of the nativity. The congregation of deceased men and women would respond to the religious worship with great fervour. Then they would leave the cemetery to go look around their village and their old homes one last time, before quietly filing back into their coffins.

Another wondrous tale from Quebec folklore described how farm animals magically gained the power of speech at the stroke of midnight on Christmas Eve. However, farmers who wanted to eavesdrop on the animals' conversations might have been disappointed, as the animals were not necessarily rejoicing on that night. In fact, more often than not they were complaining about their living conditions. The cows, horses, and sheep in the barn could be heard talking in a plaintive tone about how their hay was dry and there were hardly ever any oats to eat. Some of the animals bemoaned their lack of freedom. They remembered how they used to frolic gaily in the meadows in the days before they had harnesses and chains about their necks.

Finally, French-Canadian storytellers sometimes told the men, women, and children huddled around the fireplace that untold riches were revealed at Christmastime. Apparently, on Christmas night, the sands on the shore, the rocky hillsides, and the deep valleys would all split open, and anyone who dared to go and look could see amazing treasures shining in the moonlight.

After imparting these tidbits of Christmas lore, the storytellers would launch into the creative retelling of a holiday legend. "The Legend of Tom Caribou" and "The Legend of the Chasse-Galerie" have been passed down to successive generations of Quebecers by the oral tradition. Both legends take place at logging camps. This is not pure coincidence. Dozens of Quebec legends are set in logging camps because the men who worked in these camps were passionate storytellers.

The Legend of Tom Caribou
There were 15 men working at a small logging camp near Ottawa: the boss, the clerk, the cook, and 12 labourers. They were all great guys — they didn't argue, they didn't curse. Of course, they all had a little drink of whiskey from time to time, but they never got too drunk.

There was one fellow from Trois-Rivières, however, who really liked to drink. When he had a bottle in front of him, he just became a funnel. Tom Baribeau was his name. The Irish foreman couldn't pronounce the "Baribeau" part very well, so the men gave him a nickname — Tom Caribou.

He was a scoundrel; that was for sure. And he was a lazy bum. He talked to the devil, blasphemed the good Lord, renounced his parents five times a day, and hardly said any prayers. He sure didn't look like the kind of fellow who would go straight to heaven.

Some of the men at the camp claimed they had seen him roaming around like a *loup-garou* (a man who has turned into a beast because he's neglected his religious duties or has openly communed with the devil). Indeed, Caribou was often seen on all fours, but he never ran like the *loup-garou*. He was always too drunk for that.

Once, one of the loggers, Titoine, saw Tom climbing out of a tree. Upon reaching the ground, Tom grabbed Titoine and threatened to rip out his guts if he ever told anyone at the camp about the tree. Titoine told the other loggers what happened anyway, but the men kept it a big secret.

Every night after dinner, Tom went off on his own. He always turned his back as he was walking away to see if anyone was following him. After he was out of sight, everyone would try to guess where the rascal had gone. The men knew that he hadn't gone off on a *chasse-galerie* (a flying canoe driven by the devil), and he certainly hadn't gone to say his prayers. Strangely, Tom reeked of *rhum* every morning, even though there wasn't a drop of alcohol in the camp.

One day, shortly before Christmas, a group of neighbouring lumberjacks heard there was going to be a midnight mass somewhere in the woods. Apparently a missionary who was in the area to help the Nipissing peoples was prepared to sing the Christmas mass.

A group of loggers from Tom Caribou's camp really wanted to attend. They hadn't seen the baby Jesus or angels or any of those things for months! Of course, they weren't as bad as Tom — they didn't blaspheme the saints and insult the scriptures. But living in the woods six months of the year made it pretty hard to attend mass regularly.

On Christmas Eve, there was a full moon and the snow

was just right for snowshoeing through the woods. A group of men decided that if they left right after dinner they would probably arrive in time for the mass. Then they would return to camp in time for breakfast the next morning.

Tom had no intention of going to midnight mass. When some of the men asked him about it, he slammed down his fist, said that he couldn't care less, and then unleashed a torrent of swear words. There was no way anyone was going to try to convince him to go.

The foreman told Tom that he could stay behind and watch over the camp. Then he added, "You may not want to see the good Lord tonight, but I hope you don't see the devil instead!"

The men set off into the woods on snowshoes, each of them carrying little bags with tobacco and dry biscuits. It was an excellent nighttime adventure — walking alongside the river on fresh, light snow with the stars above. One logger began to sing his favourite Christmas hymn, *Nouvelle Agréable*, and he imagined that the bells of his own parish church were ringing and calling him to worship.

He had this strange sense that he was back home, and that his father's horses were right behind him with their manes flying freely in the wind and the little bells on their harnesses tinkling gently. But then, when the men arrived at the midnight mass in the woods, he remembered where he was.

That impromptu midnight mass was really not an

elaborate affair. The missionary was not well set up for a proper mass like the kind everyone was used to back home. The altar dishes were not highly polished, the cantors did not sing like proverbial nightingales, and the assistant who helped with the mass really looked like he would be more comfortable swinging a pickaxe than handling an incense burner. And there wasn't even a little wax baby Jesus. Without baby Jesus, what kind of midnight mass can you have, anyway?

The men had tears in their eyes. Even though it was the most rustic set-up they had ever seen for a mass, it was so beautiful just to hear those Christmas songs that most of the men had to look away so that they wouldn't cry.

Right after the mass was over, the men began the return trip to the logging camp. It was a long journey, and by the time they spotted the cabin in the distance, it was already daybreak.

The men were a little surprised to see that there was no smoke coming out of the chimney. Then they noticed that the cabin door was wide open. They went inside and discovered that the wood stove was cold and that Tom Caribou was nowhere to be found. Their first thought was that the devil had finally taken him.

The men decided that they should at least look around for the scoundrel. The search, however, would be difficult because it hadn't snowed for a while and there were dozens of tracks all around the cabin — finding Tom's tracks among them would be nearly impossible.

The boss suggested that the men take his dog, *Polisson*. So off they went into the woods with a loaded gun and the dog sniffing the ground, wagging his tail wildly. They had barely been walking two minutes when the dog suddenly stopped and began to tremble like a leaf. One of the men raised his gun and walked in the direction the dog was pointing.

Soon he spotted Tom Caribou, stuck in the fork of a wild cherry tree. Tom was as white as a sheet and his eyes were practically jumping out of his head. A mother bear was holding on to the tree, two feet below him. The loggers were not scaredy-cats, but when they saw that bear, the blood nearly froze in their veins!

The men knew this was no time to hesitate — it was the bear or them. And no one wanted to get massacred by a bear. So one of them picked up the rifle and shot two bullets into the bear's chest. The animal groaned, let go of the tree, and fell on its back, dead.

The men then saw another creature tumble out of the tree — Tom Caribou, senseless, with a massive scratch mark on his face and a chunk of flesh missing from his bottom. His hair was completely white. Fright had aged him in an instant. He was barely recognizable.

The loggers made a stretcher out of sticks, picked up Tom, and carried him back to the camp. Next, they hauled away the bear. The men noticed that the bear smelled so strongly of alcohol that some were even tempted to lick the dead animal. Tom, the rascal, had never had sweeter breath! When Tom regained consciousness, he told the others what happened. On Christmas Eve, while most of the men were at midnight mass, Tom Caribou had had some kind of private party. He had hidden a bottle of whiskey in the fork of a wild cherry tree. At one point, he'd tried to pour himself more whiskey, but was already so drunk that the spirits just spilled all over the place — and onto the sleeping mother bear.

The bear had licked its chops sleepily, wondering why the rain had such a curious smell. But when the animal blinked, the whiskey poured right into its eyes. It yelped from the stinging sensation, and from being so rudely awakened from hibernation.

With a raging mother bear on his tail, Tom had leapt into the fork of the tree. Slowly, the whiskey had taken effect on the angry bruin, and she'd hung onto the tree in a mild stupor. Tom, trembling in fright, had crouched in the fork.

Poor Tom Caribou. It took about three weeks to get him back on his feet because he had so many wounds. He was convinced that the devil himself had inflicted the injuries.

Tom looked pitiful, sitting there covered in white plasters — like a doughnut rolled in white sugar — asking everyone, including the dog, to forgive all of his tomfoolery and his swearing.

Anyway, the men knew, and Tom Caribou knew, that his meeting with the bear was his punishment for not celebrating Christmas with a pure heart, for not joining his fellows at midnight mass in the woods.

Cric! crac! cra!

Sacatabi, Sac-à-tabac!

That's the end of the story!

The Legend of the Chasse-Galerie

Joseph Ferrand worked at a logging camp on the Gatineau River one winter and he worked non-stop — felling trees, loading the logs onto sleighs, and then helping the horses get the wood out along the icy logging roads. Every night was pretty much the same as the night before. He had a simple dinner of beans and pork with the boys and then, exhausted, fell asleep as soon as he landed on his hard wooden bed.

But New Year's Eve was different; Joseph and his friends had a real party. The foreman had bought a barrel of *rhum* for everyone, and some of the boys got out the fiddles and spoons. They really made merry that night. Joseph soon lost track of how many glasses of *rhum* he had drunk!

He lay down on his bed to make the room stop spinning. Then Baptiste Durand asked him if he would like to see his girl. Would he like to see Lise? Of course! All night long, Joseph had been imagining how Lise was celebrating New Year's Eve. He had imagined the fiddle music, the square dances, the steaming tourtières, but most of all, holding his girl next to him.

"Of course I want to see Lise," said Joseph. "But she lives

in Lavaltrie, more than a hundred leagues away. It would take weeks to walk there."

Baptiste Durand assured Joseph that they could travel to Lavaltrie in a couple of hours and that they would be back by six o'clock the next morning. Then Baptiste mumbled something about taking a canoe.

"You mean a *chasse-galerie*?" Joseph asked nervously. Other loggers had told him about this enchanted canoe operated by the devil. He wanted to see Lise — his beautiful, angelic Lise — but was he crazy enough to risk his eternal soul?

Baptiste didn't seem concerned. He was too busy chatting up other loggers who were willing to take a chance in order to be home for the New Year's Eve parties. Apparently, there had to be an even number in the canoe, so when there were seven interested men, Baptiste looked at Joseph and said, "Okay. You are number eight. Now let's go!"

Just before the loggers left the cabin, Baptiste asked Joseph to "jump in the New Year" by leaping over a barrel of lard (this was the ritual for the youngest man at camp). Joseph tried to jump over the barrel, just so the other guys wouldn't notice that something strange was going on. But he couldn't do it; he just couldn't concentrate.

Baptiste, Joseph, and two other loggers stepped outside into the freezing night. The clear, bright sky crackled with stars. There were four men from another logging camp waiting for them with long, slim canoe paddles. A birchbark canoe lay in a clearing, well lit by the full moon.

Someone shouted, "Baptiste, you steer because you know the canoe." Baptiste took the stern, and everyone piled in and took up their positions in the enchanted canoe. Baptiste stood up and looked the men straight in the eyes. He told them that they were about to take an oath to the devil and that they had better not joke. If everyone followed the strict instructions, there would not be any problems. The conditions of the trip were that the men had to abstain from swearing, drinking, and speaking the name of God. Also, they had to avoid touching a cross on a church steeple during the trip. The penalty for breaking any of these rules was almost too awful to think about.

All of the men repeated after Baptiste: "Satan, ruler of hell, we will surrender our souls to you if, during the next six hours, we pronounce the name of God or touch a cross. As long as we respect these conditions, you will transport us through the air to wherever we want tonight and then back to camp first thing in the morning."

Baptiste shouted, "Acabris! Acabras! Acabram!" Suddenly, the canoe began to float up into the night sky. It soared over the camp and across the forests of southern Quebec. It flew so fast that the frosty air felt like hundreds of tiny icicles jabbing at their faces. The men looked down in amazement at the broad mirrored surface of the mighty Gatineau River and the endless stretch of dense forest. Then they started to see clusters of little lights marking villages below. The men grew so excited thinking about the festivities there that they could practically smell the *tourtières* in the ovens!

They followed the Gatineau River all the way to Deux-Montagnes. Then Baptiste told the men that they were going to fly over Montreal and he suggested that they sing a song to pass the time. They narrowly missed hitting dozens of church steeples in Montreal as they careened through the air, belting out "*Mon pere n'avait fille que moi, Canot d'écorce qui va vole, et dessus la mer il m'envoie...*"

Finally, Baptiste announced that they were coming into Lavaltrie. He decided to land the *chasse-galerie* in his godfather's field. As soon as Baptiste said, "Bramaca, Irbaca," the canoe made a sharp turn and headed down towards a snowbank in the field. The men traipsed to the village in single file. The snowdrifts were up to their hips in some places, but they didn't care because they were already so close to their goal. They went straight to Baptiste Durand's godfather's house because Jean-Jean Gabriel usually knew if there was any dance or feast going on in the village. Unfortunately, the whole Gabriel family was out, but the hired girl who had been left in charge told the loggers that there was some kind of party going on at Batisette Augé's house on the other side of the river.

Without question, the loggers wanted to join that party. So they got back into the canoe and flew up over the river. Moments later, they saw Batisette's house all aglow. The party was in full swing, and they could even hear the fiddle music from outside the house. They hid the canoe and rushed in, seeking warmth and merriment, but most of all, the girls. Baptiste reminded everyone again not to touch a drop of spirits and not to mention the Lord's name.

Batisette threw open the door and welcomed the loggers to join the party. Everyone was happy to see them, and they pestered the men to explain how they managed to make it to Lavaltrie for New Year's Eve. Baptiste said to them, "Come on, give us a chance to take off our coats and dance. There will plenty of time to explain everything in the morning."

Joseph pushed through the crowd, looking for Lise. Finally, he spotted her dancing with another man. He couldn't blame Lise. After all, Joseph had been gone for months. He went up to her casually, as if they saw each other every day, and asked for the next dance. Lise was amazed to see Joseph, but she didn't ask any questions. She just stared at him with her gorgeous blue eyes and said that of course she would dance with him. Joseph was so content to be in her arms that he completely forgot he was risking his eternal soul just to be with her for one night. They danced for hours, lost to the world. Lise and Joseph were so enamoured of each other that they did not even notice when the fiddlers stopped playing briefly to get some refreshments.

The other boys were having a ball, too. They were happy to see women again — it had been months since they'd seen any! At one point during the evening, Joseph was sure he saw Baptiste drinking whiskey. That seemed strange, considering how many times Baptiste had warned the others not to touch spirits. But Joseph was so happy to be with Lise, he didn't really think about it.

Baptiste came around at about four in the morning and said, "We have to leave now, and don't bother with good-byes or we will attract too much attention."

The thought of leaving Lise again made Joseph feel all weak and queasy. He took a chance and told Baptiste that he was going to stay in Lavaltrie. Baptiste reminded him that if they didn't all return together, there would be trouble. Of course, he couldn't jeopardize his mates' souls. So he grabbed his coat and fled the party.

The men could all see that Baptiste was drunk. They didn't want him to steer the canoe, but Baptiste was the only one who knew the way back.

The return trip to the logging camp was hair-raising. Baptiste did daredevil acrobatics with the canoe, and a couple of times they came very close to brushing up against a cross on a church steeple. Thankfully, they never actually did. It was almost as if someone was watching out for them. Either that, or the devil didn't find their souls very attractive.

The weather had changed overnight. Now the sky was dense with cloud and the loggers could not even see the moon. Baptiste worried that he might not be able to follow the Gatineau back up to the camp. Joseph became impatient, concerned that they wouldn't be able to return before their six o'clock curfew.

Then Baptiste shouted out, "Here we are boys — home again!" They landed unceremoniously in a clump of low trees. Half of the men were upside-down in the snow, and all of them were swearing a blue streak. At first, Joseph panicked because all night long they had been told to avoid swearing. But then he realized that it was okay, because they were safely back at the camp.

The next morning, Baptiste Durand was gone. Joseph asked two fellow loggers who had travelled with him the previous night where Baptiste had gone. The boys told Joseph that they didn't know whom he was talking about.

Chapter 3
Christmas Trees and Christmas Trinkets

Big bushy balsam trees are potent symbols of Christmastime. From those who grow them to those who decorate them, people all over Quebec revel in the sight and smell of Christmas trees. For some, a whiff of balsam perfume is all it takes to conjure up vivid memories of Christmases past.

Christmas trees are big business in this province — Quebec is the top producer of Christmas trees in Canada. It is also the home of Canada's first official Christmas tree.

An Avant-garde Christmas Tree

The first Christmas tree in Canada was set up in a modest house in Sorel in 1781 — about 100 years before Quebec families embraced this tradition and more than 60 years before British families began putting up Christmas trees in their homes.

By a strange twist of fate, a German officer, Baron Friedrich Adolphe von Riedesel, was based at a British garrison in Sorel. Baron von Riedesel was accustomed to the German tradition of setting up a Christmas tree on December 25. Unbeknownst to him and his family, the tree they would set up that year would have historical significance.

The Riedesel family had probably decorated a Christmas tree in their home every holiday season until they travelled to North America. Like other aristocratic German families, the Riedesels would have harvested a tree from their own forest and then decorated it with candles and a variety of natural or handcrafted items, such as paper roses, nuts, apples, gingerbread, and stars formed from straw or gold foil.

Baron von Riedesel first arrived in North America in 1776. He did not have many opportunities to think about Christmas trees and other holiday festivities during his first five years there, however, because of his military service, which included, for a time, a stint as a prisoner of war.

In 1775, American forces were in revolt against their British rulers. Apart from the riotous activity in the United States, these forces also invaded British-ruled Canada. *Les Bastonnais* (as the New Englanders were called) occupied Montreal and laid siege to Quebec City during the 1775–76 invasion of Quebec. King George III of England worried that he did not have sufficient British troops to defeat the rebellious Americans, so he called on his German allies.

In the spring of 1776, German officer Baron von Riedesel, commander of the Brunswick regiment, sailed from Portsmouth with his mercenary army of more than 4000 soldiers. His wife, Baroness Frederika Charlotte von Riedesel, and their children crossed the Atlantic soon thereafter. Unfortunately, by the time the German soldiers arrived, the American threat to Quebec was considerably reduced, so the Germans were garrisoned with some local inhabitants who lived in a strategic area south of the St. Lawrence River, between Chambly and Trois-Rivières. There they waited for the next military opportunity.

In 1777, Riedesel was involved in an offensive action at Saratoga, New York, which ended in a resounding defeat of the British forces (and their German allies). Riedesel's wife and children, along with a few other officers' families, had been travelling with the British army troops. Following the defeat, the British and German soldiers and the officers' families tried to escape. The baroness later recorded the attempt in her journal:

"Profound silence had been recommended to us; large fires were lighted, and many tents were left untouched, to conceal our movement from the enemy. We proceeded on our way the whole night. Frederika (her daughter) was afraid, and began to cry: I was obliged to press a handkerchief to her mouth."

The baroness was so courageous during this terrifying

episode that one of the British army officers said it was a pity she was not their commanding general.

Following the British army's surrender, the troops, along with the officers' families, were held as prisoners of war. The baron and his family were treated quite well while they were held prisoner. They were sent to Cambridge, near Boston, where they were accommodated in an abandoned mansion. "[The Americans] greeted us and seemed touched at the sight of a captive mother with three children," wrote the baroness.

But while Riedesel's family fared relatively well, his troops, who were held in barracks on Winterhill, suffered greatly. The barracks were extremely crowded and the soldiers were barely sheltered from the cold and rain.

Finally, in October 1780, the baron was freed during a prisoner exchange. His first assignment after his release was to command British troops who were defending Long Island. However, the baron had so much trouble dealing with the summer heat of Long Island that he requested a transfer back to Quebec.

In 1781, Quebec was still vulnerable to future attacks from the Americans, so Frederick Haldimand, the governor of Quebec and commanding general of the troops in Canada, decided to station Baron von Riedesel in Sorel, a strategically placed town at the juncture of the Richelieu River and the St. Lawrence River. Riedesel had command over the area through which the Americans were most likely to arrive.

In the middle of September 1781, the baron, his wife, and their four girls — Augusta, Frederika, Caroline, and America — arrived in Quebec City after a gruelling eight-week sea voyage along the eastern seaboard from New York City. The baroness, her children, and their servants stayed with a local family in Quebec City for a month, as there was no accommodation ready for the family in Sorel. They dined every night with Governor Haldimand. Then the family moved to Sorel and lived temporarily with a local inhabitant so that they could be closer to the baron's headquarters.

In mid-November, Governor Haldimand bought the *Seigneurie* of Sorel in the name of the British crown and acquired a house near the Richelieu River that was under construction. The foundation of the house was finished and the main walls had been erected. Haldimand instructed engineers and artisans from the Sorel garrison to ready the house by Christmas.

The Riedesel family was absolutely thrilled when they finally moved into their charming new house a few days before December 25. On Christmas Day, the family invited some British officers from the Sorel garrison to join them in their home.

"To our great surprise we were able to eat our Christmas pie — with which the English always celebrate Christmas — in our new house, although the timber for the building was felled and sawed into boards only after our arrival. Pretty paper was hung on the walls, and we were really very well lodged," the baroness wrote in her journal.

The *Maison des Gouverneurs* (as it is now called) had a very large entrance hall with benches on either side where six guards slept by turns to protect Baron von Riedesel from being kidnapped. It also had a large, stout, wood stove, which heated the house, as well as a large dining room, a spacious sitting room, and a series of bedrooms for the Riedesel family, including a nursery for the younger children. Upstairs, there were two large rooms for the male and female servants as well as two guestrooms.

The house would not have had many Christmas decorations, due to the family's recent arrival. However, on December 25, there was a handsome Christmas tree standing tall and proud in the sitting room. Shortly before Christmas, the homesick baroness had requested that her husband fetch an evergreen tree from the surrounding forest so that the family could enjoy this German tradition on Christmas Day. Evergreen branches, an ancient symbol of faith and hope, must have appealed to this transplanted German family in the rugged Canadian backwoods.

The Riedesels had a lot to celebrate on December 25, 1781: the family was reunited and safely back in Canada, they had just moved into a lovely new home, and, of course, it was Christmas! While not many details are known about the festivities that took place that evening, we do know that they included several different cultural traditions, including the British tradition of plum pudding, the French-

Canadian tradition of cranberries cooked with maple sugar, and, of course, the German tradition of an illuminated Christmas tree.

This first tree in the *Maison des Gouverneurs* was decorated very simply. There were small white candles fastened to the branches with special pins or wax, and there may have been a few star-shaped cookies.

It is easy to imagine the Riedesel children's delight as the little white candles were lit one by one and the whole room began to glow with the warm light. Gazing up at the pretty lights and breathing in the rich balsam perfume surely made the family nostalgic for their ancestral German home. The officers who were dinner guests on that Christmas night also shared in the magical scene; they were witnessing their first Christmas tree ever. They may have heard of the Christmas tree tradition from their peers, but they were probably as amazed as the Riedesel children to actually see the decorated tree.

Interestingly, the Riedesel family Christmas tree in Sorel did not start a new trend in Canada. In fact, the second Christmas tree in Canada (put up 65 years later in Halifax) was also set up to satisfy the desire of a homesick German woman. Decades after the Christmas tree tradition was introduced in Britain (1841), bourgeois Quebec families began to decorate small evergreen trees placed on tables. In 1896, a wealthy Montreal family set another precedent by using electric lights to illuminate the Christmas tree instead of the traditional candles.

Then in 1910, the popular department store Paquet mounted a display of Christmas trees adorned with garlands of electric lights. Around this time, many Quebecers began to decorate Christmas trees in their homes with imported glass balls and ornaments. Most Quebecers also incorporated a religious element into the Christmas tree tradition by placing a *crèche* at its base.

Rearing Christmas Trees

Every year just before Christmas, as he was growing up, Lucien Lapointe, along with his brothers and his father, went off in search of the perfect Christmas tree. They would traipse for hours through the woods on the Lapointe family's vast 100-acre property in the Eastern Townships. Each time one of them chose a tree, he would have to argue its relative merit, and if he couldn't convince the others, then they would all plod off again through the dense forest. Finally, after the Lapointe men came to an agreement, Dad would chop down the tree and the children would drag their trophy back through the snow, roughhousing all the way.

Lucien grew up during the Great Depression, so his childhood Christmases were very simple affairs. "No one had any money. People hardly bought anything, they were just getting by," he remembered. "We received stockings with fruits, like bananas, oranges, and a few candies. And we received one or two small presents, like a handmade wooden toy"

Harvesting Christmas trees, Richmond, Quebec, 1926.

However, Lucien did not feel deprived in any way, because his favourite part of the Christmas celebration was the annual hunt for the family tree. He did not know as a boy that he would eventually operate a vast Christmas tree business, but he did know that he had a special rapport with trees. He felt truly at home while walking through the forest, breathing in the rich perfume of the balsam fir.

Once the carefully chosen Christmas tree was brought back to the house, the Lapointe family would set it up and decorate it with a few knitted wool ornaments and a few glass balls "from the store." The traditional wooden crèche, which Lucien's father had constructed, would then be placed underneath the tree.

The tree stood at the centre of numerous family parties during *Les Fêtes*.

Like most traditional families in Quebec in the 1930s, Lucien had a huge extended family, so inviting the relatives over meant an instant party. The more the merrier. After all, there wasn't much to do on the farm during the winter months, so it was an ideal time for social visits. And Lucien loved these gatherings: "I remember trying to avoid bedtime because it was so exciting to see the house overflowing with people dancing. My father played both the violin and the piano."

After a few glasses of whiskey and some conversation about harvests, the dancing would begin. Lucien's father led the dancers through square dances, followed by jigs and reels. While the family elders played cards and Lucien and his siblings slumbered upstairs, young couples danced the night away.

Many years later, when he was a strapping young man of 15, Lucien began to formulate his first vision of operating a Christmas tree farm. His father had just acquired a piece of land near the homestead and he asked his sons to help him plant trees on a section of the land that was bare.

"We had to plant 3000 white spruce seedlings in the

forest to produce wood for construction. It was very tough, because there was hardly a proper path to get to the site and we had to carry in all of our stuff on our backs. We had branches jutting out in our faces, and there was so much water on the path that we were practically walking through a stream. It was back-breaking work, but I was absolutely in heaven!"

Lucien decided then and there that he would make his living tending trees. The only problem was money. He had to put his dream on hold to earn some money in order to buy a piece of land. So, in the early 1950s, he studied carpentry and construction in the nearby town of Sherbrooke. That course led to office jobs in Sherbrooke and then Montreal.

"But the trees were always on my mind," he remembers.

Lucien never really felt comfortable in the city, but he plodded on because he knew that eventually he would have enough money to buy his own plot. He was so ill at ease living in Montreal that he did not even drink water from the tap — it didn't taste right to him. Then, in 1969, Lucien attended a meeting of the Vermont Association of Christmas Tree Growers.

"The field was just taking off," he recalled. "I didn't know anything about growing Christmas trees, but I was very excited."

Christmas trees had always been a profitable sideline for Quebec farmers who could cut down wild balsams on their land and then sell them. Then, around 1960, the notion of growing cultivated Christmas trees on plantations became popular. Quebec is currently the top producer of Christmas trees in Canada. Each holiday season, Quebec Christmas tree producers harvest about 1.5 million trees, worth $45 million.

Lucien knew beyond a shadow of a doubt that he would grow his first plantation in the Eastern Townships as the high sloping ground and heavy soil typical of this area are ideal for growing balsam firs. And Lucien also knew that balsam firs were the most popular Christmas trees because they don't lose their needles easily and, more importantly, they boast a heady scent that smells like Christmas.

In 1970, Lucien bought his first piece of land near the Lapointe family homestead in Bury. He took seedlings from the nearby forest and transplanted them onto the field. "The neighbours weren't so happy about me planting trees on that land," Lucien recalled with a laugh. "After all, their ancestors had almost broken their backs clearing the land for agriculture."

Two years later, Lucien bought another piece of land that had belonged to his father and he was well on his way to becoming a Christmas tree grower. Despite a few setbacks due to financial problems and insects that attacked the trees, Lucien Lapointe's plantations have continued to thrive.

Taking care of the Christmas trees is extremely labour intensive. But, for Lucien, it is a labour of love. "All of the trees are beautiful, each tree is different, just like humans," he mused.

Each spring, Lucien transplants seedlings to a field. Then, at two years old, the trees are moved to another field, and at five years old they are moved again. Apart from moving trees around, Lucien and his aides are continually fertilizing the soil, clearing away weeds, pruning the trees to achieve the perfect shape, and dealing with insects and rodents that attack the bark and the foliage. Shortly before Christmas, the trees are graded, chopped down, shaken to remove dead foliage, baled, and shipped out by truck. The trees are perishable, so they cannot stay in transit for a long time.

After about 13 to 15 years of intensive care, Lucien's trees are sold in Christmas markets for about $5 per foot. Managing a Christmas tree plantation is certainly not an easy way to earn a living, but even at the age of 69, Lucien has no intention of stopping work in the fields or the Christmas markets.

"Living with trees is my life," he said.

The Christmas Lady
Every year by mid-November, Lise de l'Étoile switches into Christmas mode. It's not because she is determined to have her wreath up before her neighbours that Lise starts so early; it's because she actually *needs* more than three weeks to set up all of her Christmas decorations.

When December 25 rolls around, Lise's modest bungalow in Windsor (a small town in the Eastern Townships) is positively stuffed with Christmas paraphernalia. Her collection of Christmas decorations, which she has amassed over the last 40 years, is so extensive that she has to admit — tearfully — that maybe next year there will be no room to add new items. This would indeed be sad because most of Lise's friends and family give her Christmas-related trinkets for her birthday and for Christmas. After all, that's all she really wants.

The first step of the Christmas transformation involves clearing off all of the bookshelves, taking down framed pictures, and basically removing everything from the main floor of the house except for large pieces of furniture. Then Lise's husband, Georges, brings the precious boxes of Christmas stuff down from the attic, and Lise gets to work.

The small kitchen becomes Christmas Central. Lise fills the cupboards with Christmas-themed plates, bowls, coffee cups, wineglasses, water glasses, and serving dishes. Lise and Georges host 20-odd social gatherings during the Christmas holiday season, and Lise clearly believes that her traditional *tourtière* and *ragoût* taste better if they are served on special holly leaf dinner plates with matching glasses. For the in-between nights, when the couple is not busy preparing holiday food, they use the other Christmas china set — dishes decorated with a poinsettia motif.

Why stop at the dishes and glassware? Lise has zero tolerance for non-Christmas items in her kitchen. So, from November to January, her regular tea towels, fridge magnets, salt and pepper shakers, cheese knives, and flour and sugar canisters are all replaced with their Christmas counterparts. Anything that cannot easily be replaced is lovingly adorned with a big red bow.

Lise remembers buying her first ornaments at a Boxing Day sale in 1963, shortly before her marriage. "I just figured that newly married couples don't have a lot of money for frivolous things, so I got some simple Christmas ornaments to put in my hope chest."

Then her decoration habit just took off. "I am not sure why," she said with a smile, "I just decorate the house for Christmas because it gives me so much pleasure."

Lise wraps up every door like a present, decorates the walls with quilted candy canes, and replaces table lamps in most rooms with miniature Christmas trees that have teeny tiny lights. She even adorns the antlers of caribou and moose heads with ornaments and bows.

Then there are the music boxes! From the snowman that sings Christmas carols when the front door is opened, to a toy carousel of Christmas deer, Lise's Christmas Land home has its own soundtrack. There are also two music boxes in the dining room that are triggered by loud noise. If dinner guests get carried away while eating their soup with Christmas-tree-shaped pasta, a musical Santa starts to sing Christmas songs in French, and a musical bear sings Christmas songs in English.

"It gets pretty loud when they are both singing at the same time," she admitted.

It takes Lise almost an entire day to set up a special evergreen archway between the dining room and the living room. First she arranges the artificial evergreen boughs and then she decorates the archway with every conceivable Christmas trinket, including bells, miniature snowmen, golden stars, and candy canes.

Lise has received hundreds of Christmas-themed presents in the last 40 years and yet, incredibly, she has almost never received the same Christmas item from different people. The other odd aspect of her gifts is that Lise has often been given the mate to a present that she already had. For instance, Lise had a Santa Claus cookie jar and then a friend of hers gave her a matching Mrs. Claus cookie jar without prior knowledge of the first jar.

Lise sets up a lovely, simply adorned Christmas tree in her living room, and then she prepares a tinsel-showered "enchanted forest" of Christmas trees downstairs. Around December 4, Lise decorates at least six real Christmas trees in a corner of the finished basement. After all, when you have an international collection of almost 700 ornaments, you need more than one tree! Far from being a chore, unwrapping each of the precious decorations — which include Russian folk art and pear-shaped glass balls from Italy — and placing them on the appropriate branch is in an immense pleasure for Lise; a pleasure that she would rather not share.

"One year, my stepson offered to decorate a Christmas tree in order to help with holiday preparations. After he was

Lise de l'Etoile creates a Christmas village scene
at the base of her "enchanted forest".

gone, I took down all the ornaments he had arranged and put
them up properly," she recalled.

Lise does not put electric lights on the trees for safety
reasons; however, she does illuminate an elaborate country
village scene at the base of the trees. Lise sets up the village
scene with as much affection as a little girl setting up her
dollhouse. She places deer by the edge of a stream so they
can drink water, places a train on the tracks just beyond the
village station, and even sends skaters off for a little waltz on
the pond.

61

Lise takes down all of her Christmas decorations by mid-January.

"I would leave them up till Easter if I could, but some friends and neighbours already think that I am pretty wacky to leave them up past New Year's Day."

Chapter 4
Santa Claus Arrives

Santa Claus has been a magical bearer of gifts during the holiday season since his arrival in Quebec around the mid-19th century. During the first few decades following his arrival, Quebec children expected Santa Claus to arrive on New Year's Eve and not Christmas Eve, because December 24 was primarily a religious event. Now, Quebec children, along with other Canadian children, expect Santa's arrival on Christmas Eve. Santa Claus makes an appearance in numerous Quebec Christmas stories, as a purveyor of love and magic.

Santa Brought a Doctor's Kit
It was snowing on New Year's Eve. Giant snowflakes resembling perfectly formed crystals floated down gently, piling up

on top of each other until it looked like billowy clouds had fallen to the earth. Mont-Ste-Hilaire (just east of Montreal) and all of the surrounding countryside was soon blanketed with the pure-white mounds of snow.

Dr. Ernest Choquette was used to working at all hours — that was simply the life of a country doctor — but he was still surprised that on that New Year's Eve, at the tail end of the 19th century, someone was knocking on his door. The evening was so magical that Dr. Choquette could hardly believe someone in his community was suffering.

An elderly woman was at the door, covered from head to foot with the soft new snow. She accepted Dr. Choquette's hospitality immediately and entered the sitting room, where she almost collapsed on a parlour chair. After she caught her breath, she was able to explain why she had come out and walked across several fields during a snowstorm.

Dr. Choquette had treated the old woman's husband, as well as her daughter, numerous times, and the old woman had never been able to pay for the doctor's services. She was obviously embarrassed to ask Dr. Choquette for another favour. The doctor patiently encouraged her to talk and to explain the nature of the problem. He knew why she hesitated to tell her story. She was a very honest and very poor woman. Moved by the old woman's love and dedication to her family and her willingness to risk rebuff for them, Dr. Choquette was genuinely saddened to see this loving grandmother in such a desperate state on New Year's Eve — a night normally reserved for festivity and exchanging gifts.

Finally, he asked her if her grandson was sick, and the floodgates opened. Yes, she replied right away, he had become sick all of sudden. She explained how her grandson had gone to school as usual, but when he'd arrived home in the afternoon, he had developed a very high fever. The boy had been transformed — he lay in bed screaming out in agony and he appeared to be having terrifying dreams

As her grandson suffered, the old woman had come up with a possible explanation for his raving. On Christmas Day, Santa Claus had brought beautiful trees — the boughs laden with brightly coloured presents — to the homes of her grandson's English classmates. The children had brought their new toys to school the next day. Her grandson had been absolutely devastated because *Père Noël* had never brought him a tree or any presents. The poor child was going mad trying to understand why Santa Claus had forsaken him, and he had worked himself into a frenzy.

The old woman had tried to cheer up her grandson by going out to the woods and chopping down a little evergreen tree. However, the only things with which she'd had to decorate the tree were apples and acorns. Her sick grandson had not been at all interested in this little tree that she'd set up for him and had continued to moan about how *Père Noël* did not love him.

After she explained the situation to Dr. Choquette, the old woman suggested that maybe the doctor could provide her with some of the medicine that her neighbour's boy, Louison, had been prescribed recently. The doctor, however, knew that there was really only one appropriate response — to make a house call to see her sick grandson.

The old woman's radiant smile was the only reply that Dr. Choquette needed. She was overjoyed to hear that the doctor was willing to examine her grandson and find out what ailment was tormenting her darling boy.

While they waited for the doctor's horse and carriage to be readied for the journey, Dr. Choquette secretly went over to his children's tree, which was decorated for New Year's Day. He removed some of the toys and candies that were hanging from the branches. The doctor then sorted through the toys his children had received the year before and he chose a few items that were still in good condition, including a puppet, a music box, and a mechanical horse. As he looked at his children's toys thrown pell-mell into the toy chest, he couldn't stop thinking about the fact that the old woman's sick grandson had never received a present from *Père Noël*.

They set off in the carriage, bundled up under buffalo pelts. The snowstorm had abated somewhat, however the horse balked at the huge snowbanks and the slippery conditions underfoot. The old woman's cottage was only a few miles away, but due to the difficult weather conditions, the journey took almost twice as long as usual.

Finally, they arrived at the humble cottage, which was built up against a rock-face. Just before they entered the house, Dr. Choquette pulled some cotton batting out of his little black bag and twisted it into his mustache and beard. Then the doctor pulled up the collar of his fur coat, which was speckled with fresh snow, and took hold of the bag of presents.

As the old woman led the doctor to the sick boy's room, she turned and gave him a beatific smile. Not only had the doctor brought medicine to relieve her grandson's suffering, he had brought some magic.

When Dr. Choquette entered the little room, the sick boy sat up startled. He could not quite believe his eyes. Was it really *Père Noël*? Was he dreaming? Was his family no longer poor? His face flushed with fever, the young boy turned to his grandmother with a look of disbelief. He wanted her to say what was going on, but was afraid that he might break the spell and that *Père Noël* and all of the toys would disappear. He kept looking to his grandmother for some kind of explanation, so finally, Dr. Choquette began to speak with the sick boy in a most gentle tone. He asked the boy about where it hurt the most and whether he had been able to sleep, and suddenly the boy looked convinced.

The doctor knew the boy's belief that the legendary *Père Noël* was really standing beside him in his bedroom was due as much to his feverish state as to the doctor's convincing impersonation.

Père Noël began to examine the boy's chest and take his temperature. The boy had the glassy eyes of one hallucinating with fever. Shortly before Santa arrived, he had been tossing and turning in physical pain and emotional anguish. But now, not only was he being tended to by *Père Noël*, but he had been given magnificent toys as well. *Père Noël* must surely love him after all. As the doctor worked his healing magic, the boy relaxed and began to breathe easier.

Keeping the Magic Alive

Mme. Danielle Simard taught kindergarten in Sainte-Anne-de-Beaupré, near Quebec City, for 35 years until her retirement in 2003. She had spent dozens of Christmas seasons reading Christmas stories to her pupils, making Christmas decorations with them, and bringing them Christmas cookies. Simard had also gone above and beyond the call of duty — she'd managed to convince Santa Claus to pay a visit to her class at the École Primaire de la Place de l'Éveil for 22 years in a row. And every year, Santa had arrived in a novel way.

Once, Santa Claus had arrived all bundled up in horse-drawn carriage, like a picture out of the 19th century. On another occasion, he had zoomed in on a thoroughly modern Ski-doo. Santa had even driven a dogsled one time, calling out to the dogs like a natural.

"It depended on my whim that year, and it depended on the weather," said Simard. For instance, one year Santa Claus walked through a blinding snowstorm because that was the only means of transportation possible. It was one of the simplest plans, but it made for a very dramatic entrance.

"One time I wanted him to arrive by sleigh, but then it was raining just before the event so we had to use a car ... I really had to adapt fast," she recalled.

In December 2002, Simard enlisted the support of the local firemen and policemen for her Grand Finale. Shortly before the beginning of the Christmas holiday, the 20-odd children in Simard's class were invited to spend the night at school. The children arrived promptly at 7 p.m., wearing pyjamas and clutching their teddies or dolls. They were so excited about the upcoming evening, they appeared barely concerned about sleeping away from home.

After enjoying some Christmas entertainment in the *Grande Salle*, the children came across a note from Santa Claus: "I do not have the keys to your school, so you will have to come ou t and look for me." But it wasn't time look for Santa just yet. So the children took a little rest in their sleeping bags.

At 11:15, Simard woke the children with the jingle of little bells, and they all put on their snowsuits, mittens, and winter boots to go out and find Santa Claus. They were traipsing around the school when suddenly a police car stopped by. When the police officers heard about the children's mission, they asked if they could help out.

After pursuing several false leads, the children discovered that Santa was asleep on the roof of the school! "The children were amazed. They were looking everywhere on the ground, in the snow; then as soon as the children looked up to the roof, they were yelling and screaming with excitement that they had found him! What should we do? How will we get him down? The kids were very excited that they had found him and they were not worried about his situation," said Simard.

The children never even wondered aloud how Santa had ended up on the roof of the school. But Simard had a story just in case that question came up — she was ready to tell them that Santa's naughty reindeer had left him there as a prank.

The next step was to save Santa. The children had lots of ideas on how they might get him down from the roof. They thought of using a stepladder, but that wasn't long enough. Finally, one little girl piped up with the suggestion that they should call the fire department. Of course! Soon, a couple of fire engines arrived on the scene, and no less than six firemen helped Santa and his big bag down from the roof.

After all that hard work, Simard, the children, the firemen, the policemen, and Santa Claus were happy to go back into the school to share a little *réveillon*. Now, Simard knew that five-year-olds would not necessarily want *tourtière, cretons,* and other authentic *réveillon* dishes in the middle of the night. So her kindergarten class *réveillon* consisted of juice boxes, party sandwiches, and carrot sticks.

After their snack, Santa pulled presents out of his giant sack. "He gave them colouring books, crayons, little games; nothing was very expensive, but it was special because it came from Santa," said Simard.

The enterprising teacher persuaded the children to get back into their sleeping bags for a few more hours until sunrise. The next morning at eight o'clock, when the parents came to retrieve their children, Simard's class was filled with a joyous cacophony as each child, in turn, tried to tell their version of the previous night's events.

Remarkably, in 22 years, everything has always gone according to plan. "Children never even got homesick in the middle of the night because we started to prepare everything from the first of December," Simard explained. For instance, Santa Claus would telephone several times during the weeks leading up to his arrival. Simard would put on the speakerphone so the children could all listen to his calls. The children had oodles of questions for him — "When will you arrive?" "How will you find our school?" and "Will you bring presents?"

In the last few years, Santa Claus also sent Rudolph's harness to the children in mid-December. He told them that if they shook it around Christmastime, it would help him to find their school!

"Santa" was often one of Simard's friends, but there were a few different ones, including a professional Santa, with an appropriately round physique, who played the role in a lot of different settings, from senior citizens' homes to daycares.

"The last one was the best one," remembered Simard. "He was young, but well-built and he really put on the Santa performance extremely well and convinced the children completely ... he was almost an acrobat and the children loved that."

The annual Santa Claus visit has had a significant impact on Simard's pupils' siblings, too! Once, the mother of one of Simard's pupils called her and said that when her daughter, Véronique, had come home from kindergarten, she'd told her brother (who was in sixth grade) about how Santa Claus had telephoned that day. Apparently, Véronique had been so enthralled with the whole experience that she'd managed to convince her brother that Santa Claus really does exist.

Véronique's mother told Simard: "I could see he was really wondering about this and, while Véronique was telling the story, he asked me if it was true. After dinner, when Véronique had left the table, my son said 'Mommy, I think I believe in Santa Claus again'."

"The magic of Christmas is really there! I still wonder myself if Santa Claus exists," laughed Simard.

Chapter 5
Christmas Magic: The Art of Giving

Christmas gifts come in all shapes and sizes. They can also arrive in a variety of ways; some are delightful surprises and others are special because they have been anxiously anticipated. The simplest things can be gifts; they need only be treasured by their recipients. Some presents endure well beyond the end of the holiday season — especially those that come in the form of kind gestures and thoughtfulness.

Made With Love

Il est né, le divin Enfant!
Jouez haut-bois, résonnez musettes;

Christmas in Quebec

Il est né, le divin Enfant!
Chantons tous son avènement.

The choir sang with great affection as one more wooden sculpture was carefully placed into the Christmas *crèche*. The parishioners of St-Jean-Port-Joli (a town on the south shore of the St. Lawrence River midway between Quebec City and Rivière-du-Loup) were rapt with joy upon hearing the traditional Christmas melodies once again. They were also thrilled to view their new wooden *crèche* of human figures and animals that had all been crafted by local sculptors.

In mid-December 1987, the sculptors gave this *crèche* to the Église Saint-Jean-Baptiste as a testament of their faith and of their pride in the town's handsome 18th century church, with its fieldstone, red roof, and twin steeples. Yet the *crèche* project did not begin in solemnity — it was actually the result of a battle of wits between *curé* Sarto Lord and renowned local sculptor Benoi Deschênes.

The two men were great friends and they spent lots of time together, as Deschênes was involved in organizing a number of church activities.

"One day in December 1986, I was working on a large life-size *Christ Glorieux* (a type of sculpture portraying the Resurrected Christ) for a parish in Rivière-du-Loup. That parish wanted to have a symbolic cross above Christ's back," recalled Deschênes.

The *curé* walked into Deschênes's studio, looked up and

Church at St-Jean-Port-Joli, Quebec, 1935.

down at the work in progress, and then teased the sculptor by telling him that he shouldn't put a cross there because, after all, Christ had risen!

Deschênes had a saucy comeback ready: "I don't tell you how to give sermons so you shouldn't tell me how to create my sculptures."

The next day, Deschênes was at the parish church for a meeting regarding midnight mass preparations, and the *curé* casually inquired if he was still doing *Christ Glorieux* sculptures with crosses in the background. Deschênes happened to notice that the church's plaster Christmas *crèche* was being unpacked at that moment. The crèche had fallen on hard times — it was dusty and dilapidated, and some of the plaster figures were chipped. So Deschênes blurted out to the *curé*, "What are you doing with a plaster *crèche* in the capital of wood sculpture?"

"If you don't like our *crèche* then make us another one!" was the *curé's* simple reply.

Deschênes realized that it would be unrealistic for him to create an entirely new *crèche* for the church, so he contacted a group of his fellow sculptors. "I told them the whole story and then I said that there is no budget or anything; and they were all interested!" he recalled.

The St-Jean sculptors contacted by Benoi Deschênes had many different reasons to commit themselves to the *crèche* project. Some were moved by their Catholic faith to recreate a scene of Christ's birth on that most holy night. Others liked the fact that the *crèche* was a gift for their parish church.

Naturally, the sculptors were also motivated by the joy of friendship and collaboration. "We had worked together before for symposiums and exhibitions ... but nothing on this scale," mentioned Deschênes.

There is a rich tradition of wood sculpting in this region of Quebec. Back in the 1670s, Bishop Laval was instrumental in encouraging the teaching of arts and crafts in St. Joachim. At that time, there was a high demand for wood sculptors to decorate local churches, public buildings, and the homes of the ruling class. With the advent of mass-production, the woodcarving profession suffered a decline, although many Quebec farmers and sailors continued to carve for their own pleasure.

Médard Bourgault, a famous wood sculptor, was born in St-Jean-Port-Joli in 1897. As a boy, Médard was mesmerized by the beautifully carved, gilded wood interior of the St-Jean parish church. He spent years travelling around the world as a sailor, but in 1925, Médard realized that carving was his true vocation and so he came back to work in his father's carpentry shop. A few years later, Médard and his brother Jean-Julien opened a woodcarving studio in St-Jean. They were later joined by their brother André.

The Bourgaults were the fathers of a wood carving revival in St-Jean. Today, this small town on the south shore of the St. Lawrence River boasts 23 wood carving studios which produce many different types of sculptures, including wooden model sailboats, *habitant* farmers on snowshoes, and life-size historical figures.

When it became apparent that there was a popular interest in the creation of St-Jean's new *crèche*, the *curé* decided to open up the planning process so that any local sculptor who wanted to participate could execute one of the human figures or animals from the nativity story.

Deschênes decided to create the Joseph figure, Jacques Bourgault chose Mary, Nicole Deschênes-Duval wanted to create the infant Jesus, and Denys Heppell was interested in sculpting the gentle cow in the manger. By the end of a series of meetings, 17 wood carvers had taken on the creation of 23 sculptures.

Selecting the character was the easy part. Reality set in during the fall of 1987, when the sculptors had to complete their piece (or pieces) in time for the Christmas celebration. The main directives were that the figures had to be sculpted of linden wood, that they were to be left unfinished (not painted or varnished), and that each sculpture had to be about two feet high. Linden wood has been a choice material for European and Canadian sculptors for generations. "We wanted to use a traditional medium so that it would fit in the church," explained Deschênes.

The sculptors picked up their chisels and their wood carving knives and set to work. It was not always easy to find enough hours in the day to complete the carvings. Some sculptors also had to work on other projects simultaneously.

Nicole Deschênes-Duval had offered to sculpt the baby Jesus because she specializes in sculptures of children and adolescents. "After all the meetings and the sketches were presented it took me two to three weeks of intensive work to create the baby Jesus in his bed of straw, with a simple cover. I sculpted a baby with his eyes open and his arms and feet in the air, like a happy baby kicking his feet," she explained.

Finally, it was time to present the sculptures to the church. On December 12, 1987, the sculptors arrived with their precious woodcarvings for a special early midnight mass. (The television station Radio-Canada wanted to film the presentation so that it could be aired at Christmastime.) "Each sculptor arrived at the church with their sculpture. During the mass, the churchwardens did a little presentation of the sculptor and their creation and then each sculptor placed their own work in the *crèche*," Nicole Deschênes-Duval recalled.

The sculptures were brought to the *crèche* following the order of the nativity story. First, the gentle cow with big eyes was placed in the manger. Next came the proud parents, Mary and Joseph, and then Nicole brought the infant Jesus to rest in his little bed of straw.

"The music and the Christmas carols during the presentation corresponded to the sculptures. So when I presented the sculpture of baby Jesus, *Il est né le divin enfant* was performed," recalled Deschênes-Duval.

After the babe, the shepherds were presented, and all of the other sculptures followed in the appropriate order.

Several other sculptures have been added since 1987, including a pregnant virgin who appears during advent, another shepherd, a shepherd dog, and a star. Apart from their own satisfaction at a job well done, Deschênes and the other sculptors all benefited from the *crèche* project in the form of new wood carving projects. Deschênes was even commissioned to create a complete *crèche* for the nearby town of La Pocatière.

When asked whether any of the original sculptors plan to contribute anything else to the St-Jean *crèche*, Deschênes chuckled and replied, "The next generation will do their part."

Christmas Cards Came Raining Down

The fishermen, trappers, missionaries, and other inhabitants of the Côte-Nord were accustomed to isolation in 1927. After all, east of Portneuf-sur-Mer there were no roads connecting the dozens of little villages dotted along the north shore of the St. Lawrence River. During the summer months, when the St. Lawrence was open water, mail was delivered by boat. However, during the winter months mail was delivered by a runner on snowshoes or by dogsled. Letters often took weeks or months to arrive.

So on Christmas Day, 1927, when mailbags full of Christmas cards, presents, and New Year's wishes came tumbling out of an airplane and parachuted down to the villages along the Côte-Nord, it was like some kind of miracle. Although the Christmas mail drops were announced in the Quebec City newspapers, most villagers living on the Côte-Nord were so isolated that they had not heard about the new airmail service.

L'Action Catholique, a Quebec City newspaper, reported the event the next day: "The first airmail delivery of letters and parcels to destinations on the North Shore occurred yesterday, Christmas Day. The letters and parcels were dropped in mailbags, which were attached to parachutes. The first plane G-CAIP of the Canadian Transcontinental Airways left Lac Sainte-Agnès, near LaMalbaie at 10:15 yesterday morning and it successfully delivered the mail to over six destinations between LaMalbaie and Sept-Îles. At 2:15 p.m., the delivery was complete and Captain (Charles) Sutton who piloted the G-CAIP with Dr. Cuisinier as a passenger had successfully completed the first flight of this kind on the North Shore."

Canadian Transcontinental Airways (CTA) was founded in Quebec in 1927. CTA's chief pilot, Charles Sutton, had recently emigrated from England. The technical director and soul of the new airline was the French aviator, Dr. Louis Cuisinier. Soon after it was formed, CTA was awarded several airmail delivery contracts from the postmaster general of Canada, including the first contract to deliver airmail on the North Shore. Her Majesty's mail would be delivered twice a week during the winter season.

Sutton began the historic Christmas Day trip at Lac Sainte-Agnès, where he loaded almost 800 pounds of mail into a Fairchild plane. The small plane was simply stuffed right up to its weight capacity. All of the letters and packages had already been neatly sorted into mailbags that could easily be attached to parachutes for delivery. Then, the mailbags were placed in the airplane cabin in reverse order to the anticipated sequence of the drop: Sept-Îles, Shelter Bay, Pentecost, Trinity Bay, Godbout, Baie Comeau, Outardes, and finally, Bersimis.

It was obvious that parachute drops were the best way to deliver the mail to avoid wasting time landing and taking off from each village, and also because there were no proper landing fields near the North Shore settlements. The main disadvantage of the mail-drop system was that outgoing mail could not be picked up at each village, so the North Shore villagers had to take their outgoing mail to a central collection spot, such as Sept-Îles.

Sutton, accompanied by Dr. Cuisinier, was flying a brand new machine for this flight — a single-engine monoplane that he had picked up in New York City a few days before. It was a beautiful machine in its day, but it was not equipped with the sophisticated cockpit instruments that are standard on modern airplanes, or with radar to help with navigation. Sutton had to rely on his own vision to guide the plane safely. And if, God forbid, he ever lost his way, there was no radio available in the cockpit to call for help.

A pilot with 13 years experience, Sutton had flown in difficult situations before — he'd flown over German lines in WWI and had some experience transporting mail in the Middle East between Cairo and Baghdad. But the North Shore of the St. Lawrence is a serious challenge for any pilot; the rugged coast has always had a reputation for nasty storms and fog as thick as pea soup. In 1534, French explorer Jacques Cartier found this region so inhospitable that he called it the "Land of Cain."

Sutton was pretty busy during his flight — cruising

along the North Shore, locating the villages that were due to receive mail-drops, steering clear of fog patches and gusts of wind, and doing his best to stay warm in –20 degree Celsius weather. And of course, he also had to help deliver the mail.

Once he located a village, he alerted the inhabitants by "buzzing them" (flying very low over their houses). Then he probably made a low-level practice pass near where the mail was supposed to land. On the second pass he would have reduced his altitude to about 50 feet and tossed the rolled-up mailbag with an attached parachute out one of the plane's windows.

Naturally, Sutton never saw the villagers' reactions as they opened their mail, but he knew he was transporting a precious cargo of sentimental illustrated Christmas cards, family letters with all of the latest news, and gaily decorated Christmas packages.

As the Fairchild neared the town of Sept-Îles, a nasty squall blew up and dampened the jubilant moods of Sutton and Cuisinier, who were nearing the end of a successful flight. As wind howled and buffeted the little plane, Sutton and Cuisinier got into a heated argument. Sutton wanted to turn back because he feared for their safety. But Cuisinier — who was acutely aware of the financial implications of this inaugural route — wanted Sutton to land the plane. The first bundle of outgoing mail was waiting at Sept-Îles and Cuisinier was determined that the inaugural voyage of this mail delivery route would be a great success. CTA had invested a lot of money in the new planes and they could not afford to lose the postal contract.

As the argument between the two men intensified, the storm outside began to build. Sutton and Cuisinier yelled at each other above the roar of the wind. Neither man was prepared to back down and they continued to argue their positions. Yet the storm was more furious than either man, and it threatened to destroy both of their lives. As the plane careened down towards the icy St. Lawrence River, Sutton and Cuisinier began to tussle. The two men were so embroiled in their fistfight that they seemed to ignore the fact that they were headed towards certain death.

Finally, Cuisinier threatened Sutton (according to some sources, the threat was at gunpoint) and Sutton managed to land the plane in the bay at Sept-Îles on a bed of broken ice. Eyewitnesses at Sept-Îles reported that the plane floated along the St. Lawrence for a bit until some fishermen noticed it and towed it to shore. After the plane arrived at Sept-Îles, it picked up the outgoing mail for the return flight.

The next day, after the storm had abated, Sutton and Cuisinier returned to the base at St. Agnès, and then Sutton stormed off. History does not reveal exactly what Sutton did after that fateful Christmas Day run. However, it seems he was angry enough that he left the province.

Barely one month after the Christmas Day incident, Sutton is reported to have completed an inaugural air-mail delivery flight in western Ontario. After a very brief career, Sutton died in a tragic accident while racing a Fokker Universal on floats at the 1930 Canadian National Exhibition in Toronto.

A couple of replacement pilots delivered the mail along the North Shore in January; and then in February 1928, Canadian aviation pioneer Roméo Vachon took over the route. Vachon said that he wanted to do in the winter what the Clarke Steamship line did in the summer when there was open water. For more than 11 years, Vachon faithfully transported Her Majesty's mail to the North Shore every winter season between December 15 and April 15. And the villagers on the North Shore soon came to expect regular mail delivery.

Christmas Shoeboxes

Graham Reynolds and André Bellerive have been playing Santa every Christmas season since 1998. But the Christmas greetings and the presents hiding in their big red sack are not for children — they are for international sailors.

Reynolds and Bellerive are volunteers at the Maison du Marin at the Port du Quebec (port of Quebec City). This centre, founded in 1850 as the Seamen's Mission, provides a host of different services for the seamen, including access to recreational activities, reading material, free clothing, and visits with a chaplain. For the last 21 years, the Maison du Marin has also provided Christmas "shoebox" presents to the crews of international ships.

At the beginning of December, Reynolds and Bellerive

start to deliver the gift-wrapped shoeboxes to the crews of ships that will either be in the Port du Quebec or out at sea on Christmas Day. After December 25, the two Santas give out boxes to ships with crews of Greek or Russian orthodox origin so that these sailors receive gifts for the Orthodox Christmas on January 6. In 2003, Reynolds and Bellerive brought 896 boxes onboard 39 different ships. "For many seamen, the present that they receive from us is their one and only present," said Reynolds.

In the fall, people all over Quebec prepare their shoeboxes for the Maison du Marin. School groups, women's church groups, nuns, and a multitude of individuals fill their boxes with about $20 worth of little gifts, such as pens, playing cards, shampoo, razors, shaving lotion, stationary, mittens, and *tuques* (woollen hats). Many donors also include a little note with Christmas greetings.

"The boats are pretty cold in the winter, so the sailors are very happy to find a scarf or a *tuque*," said Bellerive.

"And they love to receive little hand-held pocket calculators," added Reynolds. Electronic gadgets are fun novelties for sailors from developing countries.

Reading material is not usually included in the boxes, as the sailors speak a great variety of languages and there is no way of knowing where a certain shoebox is going to end up. Also, sailors can visit the Maison du Marin, to read *National Geographic* and other magazines, books, and bibles in more than 10 languages.

Christmas Magic: The Art of Giving

Before joining the Maison du Marin, Graham Reynolds worked as an electrician onboard ship. When he was approaching retirement, a friend of his, who was also the Protestant chaplain at the Maison du Marin, suggested that Reynolds help out with the shoebox delivery. André Bellerive was the director of student services at l'Université Laval prior to his retirement. Bellerive's best friend, the harbour master of the Port du Quebec, suggested that he volunteer at the Maison du Marin. Now, Reynolds and Bellerive are at the centre every morning and sometimes in the evenings or on weekends, depending on ship arrival times.

Although Reynolds and Bellerive do not dress up in Santa Claus costumes, the sailors await their arrival with the same anticipation as small children awaiting the mythical Santa on Christmas Eve. In 2003 when the two volunteers were approaching a ship, some sailors called out, "Santa Claus has come!"

Reynolds and Bellerive bring presents onboard ships that have come from around the globe — Russia, Liberia, Greece, Ukraine, and the Philippines. Of course, not all sailors celebrate the Christian holiday of Christmas, but that is not a problem. "We put some Christmas shoeboxes onboard Chinese ships, and they were just as happy to get a present as anyone else," recalled Reynolds.

"Their reaction depends on how their work is going, and sometimes on their nationality, too. The Filipinos — who are numerous in the shipping business — always have a smile and they are ready to joke. The Ukrainian crews are very thankful for the presents, but they can be quite taciturn," explained Bellerive.

Reynolds and Bellerive are delighted to be able to provide the crews with a little fun at Christmas, but they do miss the old days when they could really get to know the individual sailors who worked on charter ships that had regular routes. "They are mostly tramp ships now," explained Reynolds. "They (the sailors) never know where they are going next."

A container ship might travel to Brazil, then to Spain, then to Turkey, then to England, then to the U.S., and then to Canada. Reynolds and Bellerive almost never see the same sailors on a regular basis.

"There used to be a ship, the *Daishowa Voyager*, that came in here every three weeks for 13 years with a Filipino crew. The local pulp and paper mill had a big export for paper and chartered this ship. But now to cut down on cost, the mill just brings in ships when they need them."

The *Stolt Aspiration* is one of Reynolds's favorite ships. This Liberian ship comes to Quebec about three or four times a year to pick up tallow and transport it to ports around the world. The boat smells horrendous due to its cargo of animal fat, but the ship's crew is an extremely friendly group of men.

Of course, regardless of whether the crews have ever met the Maison du Marin volunteers before, they are always extremely appreciative. After Reynolds and Bellerive have brought the presents onboard, they are usually invited to join the seamen for some coffee, tea, or vodka, depending on the ship.

The Maison du Marin receives hundreds of letters and faxes of thanks, and sometimes the sailors are so grateful for the shoeboxes, they give the volunteers a present in return.

One time, after the volunteers brought presents onboard a Chinese ship, the chief engineer came back two days later with a model of a junk that he had made himself. It was made of bamboo and mahogany, without any nails whatsoever.

"Some people put their names and addresses in the shoeboxes and they receive a letter of thanks. One woman who prepared a shoebox even received a marriage proposal from an appreciative sailor," said Bellerive.

The Christmas shoebox project gets underway every September, when Maison du Marin volunteers send out information letters to interested individuals and organizations across Quebec. Each year, the Maison du Marin typically receives about 850 to 1000 filled boxes. Most people mail or hand-deliver their boxes to the Maison du Marin, but Reynolds also hits the road to go and pick up some boxes. Last year, he picked up about 150 boxes from the Eastern Townships and the Gaspé.

The Maison du Marin volunteers never know exactly how many boxes they will receive each year, and they cannot predict how many they will be giving out, either. Incredibly, they are almost never short of gifts.

"We give them out until they are all gone," explained Reynolds. "We used to give out the last ones around Christmas; now, we often have some left over, even after Epiphany. We don't keep any for the following year, we simply give away any extra boxes to sailors who are especially poor."

Nez Rouge

Louison Francoeur, chief dispatcher at the Montreal Opération Nez Rouge, has collected dozens of incredible stories during his 10 years as a volunteer for Nez Rouge — an organization that provides free transportation during the last three weeks of December in an effort to prevent drinking and driving.

"One time a client had forgotten to change his address on his driver's licence, so the Opération Nez Rouge team took him to his old address by mistake. You can just imagine the look on the client's ex-wife's face when she was woken up at 3 a.m. by her drunk ex-husband."

"Another time when I was a driver," he recalled, "I had a client who was getting all cozy with a male companion. Her phone was frozen, so I offered to lend her my phone. She called a number and said that she was going to sleep at Grandma's house. When I commented that it was nice of her to call her parents, she told me that she wasn't calling her parents, she was calling her boyfriend."

Francoeur was based at the Tourist Hall of the Olympic Park for a recent Montreal Opération Nez Rouge. He remembers the tremendous sense of camaraderie among Nez Rouge volunteers who turned up regularly for a twofold purpose — a sense of social responsibility as well as a desire to enjoy themselves heartily on a cold winter night. In fact, the base of operations sometimes felt like a Christmas party.

Volunteer drivers in official "Nez Rouge red" were clearly thrilled to see each other again for the first time since the previous Christmas. When they weren't busy dispatching or driving, Francoeur and his fellow volunteers enjoyed sipping coffee and regaling each other with amazing anecdotes and urban legends.

And yet the most amazing story of all is how a mathematics professor and swim coach from Quebec City has managed to help change Quebecers' attitudes towards drinking and driving.

In 1984, Jean-Marie De Koninck was looking for a new way to raise funds for his swim team at l'Université Laval. He heard a radio report about how 50 percent of fatal car accidents in Quebec were due to alcohol. It seemed that people were more reluctant to leave their cars overnight than to drive drunk.

The proverbial light bulb went off in De Koninck's mind as he realized that he could come up with a plan that might simultaneously help to reduce the level of drunk driving and fill the swim team's coffers. Opération Nez Rouge was set in motion in the fall of 1984.

De Koninck realized that Opération Nez Rouge would be an ideal name for his fundraising/road safety improvement project, but first he had to ask the Canadian forces for permission to use the name — the Canadian army was already using the term to refer to a military exercise that took place every February. (It was generally freezing cold at that time, and the soldiers' noses would turn red during the exercise.) Once De Koninck was granted permission to use the name, he designed an ingenuous model for the free transportation service.

When a call was received from a client who needed a ride, a three-member volunteer team would set off in one of the volunteers' cars. Then, after they reached the client (who was typically at a party or a bar), two of the volunteers would get into the client's car. One of those two would drive the client wherever he chose to go, while the other would keep a record of the ride and write a receipt for the tip (which was optional). Naturally, the "secretary" volunteer also played a security role. The third volunteer, meanwhile, would follow behind the client's car and then once the client had been safely escorted, all three volunteers would return to the base of operations.

In September 1984, the swim team members started to get friends and family involved as volunteers for Opération Nez Rouge. By early December, there were 200 volunteers ready to go, the Quebec City police force was helping check the volunteers' driving records, and a local radio station had offered to lend them their switchboard. Nez Rouge provided 463 rides that first year, and they raised $20,000 for bursaries for swim team members.

De Koninck had expected that Nez Rouge would be a good vehicle to raise money for his swim team, but he could never have predicted the popular appeal of this organization for Quebecers. "Following the tremendous success of the first Nez Rouge, the SAAQ (Société des Assurances Automobile de Quebec, the provincial government's no-fault car insurance program) asked Jean-Marie to make his idea available to other regions," explained Pierre-Étienne Talbot, the regional co-coordinator for Nez Rouge. "They knew that the Nez Rouge message had a lot of potential to improve Quebecers' attitudes towards drinking and driving."

De Koninck had originally imagined that Opération Nez Rouge would be a one-shot deal. However, due to its initial success, six new Nez Rouge operations were set up across Quebec — from Sherbrooke to the Outaouais region — in 1985. That year, 1700 ready volunteers provided 3513 rides.

According to Talbot, the Nez Rouge headquarters has been signing contracts with regional operations since the beginning. Today, each regional Nez Rouge is responsible for managing its own operation with the support of the local police force and a local radio station. The Nez Rouge headquarters in Quebec City provides the philosophical direction, organizes the global media campaign, and compiles statistics.

The contracts with regional operations bind them to certain requirements, including operating the Nez Rouge program exclusively in December, adhering to the three-person team model, donating the profits to a youth organization (preferably sports-oriented), and organizing a local media campaign. In return, the Nez Rouge headquarters provides each regional operation with posters and other communications materials, as well as the official red vests for volunteers.

There are currently 70 regional Nez Rouge operations across Quebec and 100 in the rest of Canada. There are even a few in European countries, including France and Switzerland.

One explanation for the astounding popular appeal of this organization is that it is non-judgmental. The volunteers do not deliver any lectures about alcohol abuse, and they will even drive a client from one bar to the next if that is where the client wants to go. (Naturally, the assumption is that the client will eventually ask for a safe drive home.) The main message of Nez Rouge is, "Make merry during the Christmas holidays — drink, eat, dance! Just don't drive if you are drunk."

Opération Nez Rouge has plenty of high-level friends. The SAAQ has been a major sponsor since 1985. Desjardins Assurances, Nez Rouge's official insurer, is a significant financial partner. A number of media partners have also been instrumental in helping Nez Rouge transmit their educational message and recruit volunteers.

There is an interesting new trend among corporations to organize volunteer nights at Nez Rouge. For instance, one night during the 2003 Opération Nez Rouge in Montreal, Labatt Brewery provided 14 3-person teams. The Montreal police force volunteer *en masse* as Nez Rouge drivers, as do Urgences Santé (Quebec ambulance service) employees. Speaking of ambulances — Louison Francoeur is convinced that Nez Rouge drivers sometimes arrive faster than an ambulance would! "One time a Nez Rouge team arrived very shortly after the client had called. The client actually told them that they were too fast and then he gave them $20 to make them go away," recalled Francoeur.

After a few intense weeks of driving clients home from Christmas parties, suddenly it is New Year's Eve (a very busy night for Opération Nez Rouge), and then it is time to wrap up the stories until next year.

Opération Nez Rouge is held only at Christmastime for three reasons, explained Talbot. "First of all, if we presented our message to help reduce the number of impaired drivers on the road all year round, it would not have the same impact. Secondly, we have wonderful media sponsors who do a real media blitz in December and if we had this campaign all year long, we probably would not have the same level of participation.

"Finally, we need about 35,000 volunteers to make it (Nez Rouge) work properly and it would be unrealistic to expect those kind of numbers if we operated all year long. And there would not have the same festive atmosphere among the volunteers."

De Koninck is encouraged by the fact that the number of rides provided by Opération Nez Rouge has dropped from 99,000 in its peak year of 1997 to 65,828 in 2003. He feels that Quebecers must be learning to anticipate their return journey when they go out to have a drink. Assigning designated drivers, as well as choosing public transportation and taxi services, are increasingly popular alternatives to driving while inebriated.

Quebecers used to be embarrassed to be seen getting a ride home from Nez Rouge. Now they are embarrassed to be seen planning to drive drunk. Nez Rouge's educational message, combined with stiffer penalties for people charged with drunk driving, has helped to improve road safety in Quebec. In the last 19 years, the fatality rate in automobile accidents caused by alcohol consumption has dropped from 50 percent to 30 percent, according to SAAQ statistics.

Chapter 6

Holiday Tales of Adventure and Survival

Most of the land in Quebec is wilderness, so it is not surprising that there are many Quebec holiday stories about great adventures and survival in the bush. Dramatic tales abound, among them: camping out in northern Quebec, 16th-century explorers coping with a mysterious illness, a natural catastrophe that interrupted a New Year's Eve party, and mayhem at a Laurentian ski resort.

Camping On Christmas Eve

Regis Sirois had just finished packing all the luggage and some Christmas presents into his Cessna 170 at about 10 o'clock in the morning on Christmas Eve, 1986. It was a bright, beautiful winter morning in Rimouski (a town on the south shore of the St. Lawrence River near the Gaspé peninsula), the kind of day when the sky is a pure royal blue and the snowbanks sparkle in the sunshine.

Regis, his wife Micheline St-Laurent, their six-year-old daughter Stéphanie, and Micheline's brother, Jean-Yves St-Laurent, were getting ready for a surprise trip to spend Christmas with Micheline and Jean-Yves's sisters in Fermont, a small town in northern Quebec near the Labrador border. "My sisters had wanted us to come for Christmas for a long time, so our big Christmas present was to go and visit them on a surprise trip," recalled Micheline.

Meanwhile, oblivious to Micheline's imminent arrival, Jacinthe and Lina were hard at work preparing traditional Christmas dishes, *tourtières* and *bûches de noël* (rolled cakes decorated to look like logs), for their own families.

The trip started out as a routine flight. Regis had been flying for more than a dozen years and he was a natural in the air. The Cessna sailed out over the outskirts of Rimouski and then over the choppy waves of the St. Lawrence River. Then the airplane began to soar over the rugged boreal forest of northern Quebec. Regis reached a flying altitude of about 5000 feet, and his passengers settled in for the four- to five-hour trip over endless forests. The incessant noise in the cabin of the small plane was hypnotic.

Though it was a glorious sunny morning, it was also very windy. In fact, the plane was heading into the wind during most of the trip, and Regis suspected that they might start to run low on fuel. Sure enough, as they were approaching the abandoned iron-mining town of Gagnonville, Regis realized that they probably did not have enough fuel to make it to Fermont. He decided to land on the old Gagnonville runway in order to get out and refuel. After all, there were not very many runways out in the bush and he did not want to chance having to fly to Fermont on fumes.

Regis landed the Cessna on the abandoned runway, disembarked, took the gas containers from the plane, and filled up the tank. Only then did he realize that the snow on the runway was very soft. Regis knew that it would be difficult to take off with the heavily laden plane in these conditions.

The family got out of the plane, put on their snowshoes, and tried stamping down the snow to make a harder surface for takeoff. That did not really work. Regis realized that they would have to let the stamped-down snow freeze overnight to make a harder surface. With a heavy heart, he informed his wife, daughter, and brother-in-law that they would be spending Christmas Eve in a ghost town.

"There wasn't much left of Gagnonville, just the old airport and the runway. All of the other buildings had been broken down and bulldozed," said Regis. "So, we just went in the old airport. We tore down pieces of wood from the ceiling and from around the windows to make a fire in a corner of the airport, and then we slept in one of the old offices."

That night, the family members huddled together in

sleeping bags and ate up the emergency rations from the plane — chocolate, chips, peanuts, and cookies. They also melted snow in a small container on the campfire to get drinking water.

"It was about –30 Celsius outside; we were not exactly cozy, but we did not feel cold," said Regis. The family did not even think about wild animals because they were so preoccupied with staying warm and managing to get a bit of sleep.

In the meantime, the local airport at Fermont noticed that Regis Sirois had not completed his flight plan. "That must have been a terrible surprise for my sisters," said Micheline. "They did not even know we were coming and then they got a call from the Sureté de Québec (Quebec Provincial Police) to inform them about rescue efforts."

Of course, Regis had a radio onboard the plane, but he could not use it to call Fermont because radio communication was only possible when the plane was in the air.

Later that night, a search and rescue plane flew over the family at Gagnonville. Regis went into his plane and achieved contact with the pilot. (The radio in the grounded plane could be used to communicate with the search and rescue plane because it was in such close proximity.) Regis told the rescue team that his family was fine.

"They noticed that we had dropped out of the sky (i.e., they were not following their flight plan) and they wanted to send a helicopter to come and help us, but finally the weather conditions were impossible for a helicopter," said Regis.

The next morning, the family tried to depart Gagnonville, but the plane still would not take off. Regis knew that it would be easier for the plane to take off if there was less weight onboard, so he asked Jean-Yves to stay in the abandoned airport until he could come back to get him. Jean-Yves accepted the request immediately to help his brother-in-law's family, but he must have been unnerved by the thought of waiting alone in the wilderness for an undetermined amount of time. After all, there were plenty of potential dangers to worry about, like severe frostbite and hungry wild animals.

Regis, Micheline, and Stéphanie arrived safely in Fermont about one hour later and were greeted by Sureté de Québec (SQ) officers who wanted to ask them all about the ordeal. When the SQ officers heard that Jean-Yves was still in Gagnonville, they recommended that Regis and his family find an alternate mode of transportation for Jean-Yves's return because a snowstorm was coming and it would be too dangerous to fly.

"So then, the brother of my sister's husband left with some friends by Ski-doo in the afternoon to go and get Jean-Yves," explained Micheline.

Meanwhile, back in Gagnonville, Jean-Yves was getting bored. He'd spent hours tending a little campfire and looking up at the sky. He kept expecting to see Regis returning in the Cessna to come and pick him up.

When the weather turned and vast amounts of snow began to fall, Jean-Yves realized that he was in the midst of a major snowstorm and that Regis probably would not be flying back to Gagnonville after all. Jean-Yves just had to trust that somehow, someone would be coming to get him. It started to get dark and Jean-Yves began to mentally prepare himself for another night in the abandoned mining town.

Finally, at around 11 p.m., "about four snowmobiles with my brother-in-law's brother, plumbers, Fermont firemen, and a whole bunch of great guys came to pick me up," recalled Jean-Yves.

They spent more than six long hours getting back to Fermont by snowmobile because the travelling conditions were horrendous. "The snow was no good — it was granular — and that can double or triple your travelling time on a snowmobile. It took a long time to rescue Jean-Yves," remembered his sister Micheline.

Then, as dawn broke in the little town of Fermont, Jean-Yves joined Regis, Micheline, and Stéphanie at his sister's house, and the whole extended family was able to contemplate how they wanted to spend the rest of their Christmas holiday!

Christmas 1535

Jacques Cartier's first Christmas in Canada was a nightmare. After exploring the St. Lawrence River and its shoreline, Cartier and his band of 110 men prepared to be the first European explorers to over-winter in Canada. These adventurers were brave, hardy souls with no fear of discomfort.

They had experienced chilly weather before in France, but nothing prepared them for the hell they would experience during the winter of 1535.

In early September, Cartier and his crew reached Canada (the Native term for the area around present-day Quebec City), where they were greeted by Native people who were happy to trade eels and melons for glass rosary beads and little metal knives. The Native people were also overjoyed to see the return of Domagaya and Taignoagny, young men who had travelled to France with Cartier following his first voyage in 1534.

When Cartier and his crew reached Stadacona, the main settlement in Canada, they were greeted by chief Donnacona, Taignoagny and Domagaya's father. The explorers were not invited into the Native village right away, but they were welcomed with great enthusiasm and told many fascinating tales about other Native villages, including Hochelaga (site of present-day Montreal).

The French explorers' mandate was to find riches for France and, if possible, a route to Asia. Cartier believed that the St. Lawrence River was a possible conduit to the Kingdom of the Grand Khan, so he was determined to continue upstream towards Hochelaga. He moored the expedition's largest ships, the *Grande Hermine* and the *Petite Hermine*, in a nearby river, which he called the Ste. Croix (now the St. Charles River), and prepared the *Emérillon* to sail further upstream to Hochelaga.

The Iroquois villagers from Stadacona tried to dissuade Cartier from taking this journey, claiming that the river was too dangerous upstream. Perhaps the Iroquois were also reluctant to share their generous guest, who was constantly handing out beads, trinkets, and other gifts. At any rate, just as Cartier and his men were setting out for Hochelaga, a group of Native people in frightening attire with blackened faces and horns on their heads approached Cartier's ship by canoe. They warned the explorers that their god, *Cudouagny*, had told them there would be so much ice and snow that all would perish on the journey.

Undaunted, Cartier took half of his crew and set off to visit Hochelaga anyway. Meanwhile, the rest of the crew set to work to prepare their lodging at the mouth of the Ste. Croix River. They constructed a simple wooden fort surrounded by a palisade — a fence made of stakes driven into the ground. Then the Frenchmen, who were obviously not completely at ease, inserted their ships' cannons into the palisade.

Upon his return from Hochelaga in mid-October, Cartier realized that it was too late in the year to pursue any more exploration, so the men settled into a wintertime routine at the fort. Snow began to fall, and soon the land was covered with a thick, white blanket. The north wind raced in through chinks between the logs of the walls and the men shivered in their light European clothing. The state of their larder was even more alarming — a few limp vegetables and salt meat were their sole provisions for the winter.

As the Canadian winter season began to enclose the sailors in an icy prison, they must have begun to dream about Christmas merrymaking with their friends and family back home in France.

Some men probably reminisced about the way Christ's birth was celebrated in their hometowns. At Christmastime, they might have witnessed the performance of a liturgical drama in a cathedral square. The sailors probably also had fond memories of worshipping at a *crèche*. In 16th century France, most churches and many homes boasted beautiful handcrafted *crèches*.

In addition to the spiritual aspect of Christmas, some of the sailors surely recalled the sensory pleasures of the festive season, such as bustling Christmas markets, where fattened geese and other delicacies required for traditional meals could be purchased. Some may have remembered minstrels wandering from town to town, regaling people with stories and songs about the marvels of *la sainte nuit* (the holy night).

Cartier's crew hailed from very modest homes in Brittany, so the sailors' fantasies of Christmas dinner probably featured visions of buckwheat pancakes and sour cream. Nonetheless, a simple meal of buckwheat pancakes would have been a lot tastier than the stale biscuits and salt meat the men were eating in the Canadian wilderness.

Their ships were trapped in thick ice blocks and the snowdrifts grew higher than the ships' decks. The inner walls of the small fort were soon coated with frost. To add insult to injury, all of the crew's barrels of wine and cider were frozen onboard the ships.

But the worst was yet to come. In December, Cartier noticed that some of the Iroquois from Stadacona were affected by a mysterious illness that left them so weak they could hardly stand up. The most acutely ill had swollen limbs and rotting gums. Cartier forbade the Iroquois from approaching the fort for fear that they would bring the dread disease with them. However, despite Cartier's efforts, his own men were soon afflicted, moaning and groaning with pain as their bodies began to deteriorate due to internal bleeding.

According to Cartier's journal of the expedition, "some lost all of their strength, their legs became swollen and inflamed, while the sinews contracted and turned black as coal ... then the disease affected their hips, shoulders, arms and neck and their mouths became so diseased that the gums rotted away down to the roots of the teeth, which nearly all fell out."

The disease continued to take its toll on Cartier's men, until the sick and the dead began to outnumber the healthy ones. The fort had become a haven of misery and despair, and most of the men began to accept that they might never return to France.

At this point, superstitious members of the crew may well have remembered, with a shudder, the Natives' warning prior to their departure for Hochelaga that Cartier's men would perish in the snow and ice.

Cartier clearly knew how protect his men from military attack; at the beginning of the winter, the captain had ordered reinforcements to be added to the humble fort, including deep ditches all around the fort and a solid door with a drawbridge. He had also instituted a night watch. However, confronted with this dread sickness among his crew, Cartier was completely helpless. Finally, the captain decided to draw on the crew's religious convictions.

Cartier requested all of the men who could walk to participate in a special religious procession. The pathetic men hobbled through the snow and ice, reciting the Psalms of David with quiet desperation. The chaplain performed a mass by an image of the Virgin Mary that had been posted to a tree and asked Mary to have pity on the sufferers. While some sailors might have given a passing thought to the celebration of Christ's birth, most of the prayers that Christmas were probably to ask God to spare them death in a foreign land.

When religious entreaties failed to improve the situation, Cartier ordered that an autopsy be performed on one of the cadavers in a desperate attempt to discover the cause of the horrific disease. According to the journal of the expedition, "the corpse's heart was white and flaccid, lying in a reddish water. The liver was fine but the lung was black and degraded. When the body was opened, a large quantity of black and putrid blood came out ... then we cut open the leg which was black on the outside but the flesh was fine on the inside. He has been buried with the least harm possible. God of Holy grace, forgive his soul and all trespasses. Amen."

Today we know now that this man, and all of Cartier's other men who died, were afflicted with scurvy, a disease caused by a lack of vitamin C. The sailors' meagre winter diet of preserved meat and dry biscuits was virtually devoid of this vitamin. However, the primitive autopsy did not reveal the cause of the disease that was ravaging his crew, and Cartier was at a loss.

Cartier was determined to give a show of strength to the Natives, in case they should take advantage of the French crew's weakened state. When the Natives came near the fort, Cartier came out with a few healthy crew members. The captain pretended to get mad at his men and then ordered them to do certain chores, as if the men were being lazy. He also had these men make noise inside the ships so that the Natives would assume the reason they hadn't seen the sailors much was because they were all doing maintenance onboard.

Cartier had heard that Domagaya was deathly ill with the dread disease that was ravaging the French crew. But one day, Cartier was out for a walk and he met Domagaya, who was in perfect health. Cartier wanted to ask how Domagaya had been healed, but he did not want to reveal that almost his entire crew was bedridden. So the captain claimed that he wanted to know the remedy in order to treat a servant who was ill.

Domagaya immediately sent two women to gather branches from the annedda tree (white cedar). These Native women taught Cartier to grind up a few of the branches and then to boil this powder with the annedda leaves. The women told Cartier to give this potion to the sick man every two days and to rub the dregs of the potion on swollen parts of the body.

According to the journal of the expedition: "After the Captain made the medicinal beverage, none of the sailors wanted to try it. Finally one or two took a chance and tried this drink. Soon after they drank it, they started to see the result and it was like a miracle because after drinking this potion two or three times, they started to regain their health and their strength ... they used an entire tree, one of the largest I have ever seen, in less than eight days."

Cartier and his surviving sailors returned to France in the summer of 1536.

Tragedy in Northern Quebec

As mayor of Kangiqsualujjuaq (an Inuit community near Ungava Bay in northern Quebec), Maggie Emudluk attended most of the traditional Christmas season festivities between December 23 and January 2. There were outdoor activities every day, like fishing contests and snow sculpting, and in the evenings there were indoor games and Christmas worship services in the arctic village's little Anglican church.

On December 31, 1998, Emudluk, along with about half

of the village's 650 inhabitants, were gearing up for the grand finale of the holiday season — the New Year's Eve celebration. This event was being held in the Satuumavik School gymnasium. The gym was a real focal point for the community — it was used for everything from bake sales to sporting events, and on this special night it would become a site of worship and a dance hall. Satuumavik School was the largest public building in Kangiqsualujjuaq.

The villagers started to gather in the gymnasium around 9 p.m. The gym was still decorated with children's artwork, which had been put up for the school Christmas concert a couple of weeks earlier. There were no glitzy banners or streamers festooning the gym. After all, this was not a chic urban bash. It was a low-key gathering for the entire community, from babies to elders, and they didn't need fancy decorations in order to feel festive. It was enough just to celebrate their togetherness.

There was a little canteen set up in the gym, selling pop and other snacks. Wine and beer were not available at the party because alcohol sales had been severely restricted by the town council since the mid-1990s.

The villagers slowly began to filter into the gym, joining their family and friends. "Then, at the stroke of midnight, the Canadian rangers [people trained by the Canadian armed forces to do search-and-rescue work] went outside to fire 60 or 70 shots in the air to mark the arrival of the New Year. Usually, we all went outside to see that, but that year we did not because there was such a bad snowstorm outside," Emudluk recalled.

Following the celebratory shots, there was a special Anglican worship led by one of the schoolteachers, who was also a lay preacher. The villagers celebrated an Inuktitut service, which included many rousing hymns and carols. There were also prayers for the coming year and prayers for the families of two local people who had drowned the previous fall.

Then it was time for the festivities to begin. Emudluk was eager to see what the recreation committee had organized that year. She knew there would be some form of community dance followed by games for all ages, including traditional Inuit games involving feats of strength and agility, and scavenger hunts adapted for different age groups. Dance contests, to see who could dance for the longest amount of time without tiring, were also very popular games.

But now, it was time for the traditional square dance. The accordion player was warming up, and everyone was looking for dance partners. Soon the dance was underway, and people were swinging every which way. The accordion player clearly knew which dances appealed to the crowd. Caught up in the rhythm of the music, small children darted between the adult dancers, until they were swept up into someone's arms.

The dance ended around 1:30 a.m., and it was time to award the door prizes. "I was sitting down like everyone else," said Emudluk. "We were very hot right after the dance."

Then the unthinkable happened. There was a terrific cracking sound and a mountain of snow exploded into the school gymnasium. Trucks and Ski-doos parked outside were tossed aside like playthings. An avalanche was plowing through the back wall of the gym!

The community had chosen to build the Satuumavik School very close to a small hill in order to protect the children from bitter winds. And yet, in a cruel irony, the school's proximity to the hill actually intensified the effect of the avalanche by enabling the snow to roar down into the gym at a furious speed.

The mayor was sitting with some friends about 10 feet away from the wall that came down. "Everybody did something," she said. "I do remember saving people, but there are some spots I can't remember."

Emudluk and other people who were not buried by the avalanche grabbed shovels, frying pans, and anything else they could find to dig with. Many people simply used their bare hands to rescue loved ones.

Mary Baron, the school director, was sitting with her three-year-old son after the dance. She was not completely covered by snow and was able to dig out her son in time to save his life.

Then a group of villagers ventured beyond the school to continue looking for friends and family members. For more than three hours, they battled 100-kilometre-per-hour winds and a raging snowstorm. It wasn't easy to see anything through the blizzard, but the rescuers were guided by calls of distress from people buried in the snow. The impromptu rescue team was freezing cold on that awful night in the Arctic, but they kept up the search effort. They knew they didn't have a lot of time to locate the victims before they suffocated in the snow.

The people of Kangiqsualujjuaq were used to being self-reliant. When you live 300 kilometres away from the closest hospital, you know that emergency workers can't arrive moments after an incident. So the brave villagers basically conducted their own search-and-rescue effort.

"More than 50 people were saved," said priest Benjamin Arreak, who ministers to five communities in northern Quebec. However, despite courageous rescue efforts, 25 people were injured in the avalanche crash and nine people died.

Nine hours after the avalanche, doctors and nurses arrived from the Ungava Tulattavik health centre in Kuujuuaq. Extreme weather conditions had prevented the medical personnel from arriving any earlier.

Following the incident, Emudluk explained that an outpouring of support from other villages and towns in northern Quebec helped to comfort the people of Kangiqsualujjuaq. The villagers also relied on the ancient Inuit tradition of *ayurnamat* (an Inuktitut term which means accepting things that you have no control over) in order to cope.

"That is our tradition to accept. That has helped people get past it," explained Emudluk.

There is a beautiful new teal-blue school in Kangiqsualujjuaq, now called *Ulliaraq* ("star" in Inuktitut). Children at Ulliaraq are engaged in a wide range of different activities, from learning about traditional Inuit life to playing hockey. Some of the children are even learning to play the violin via satellite video-conferencing.

The villagers of Kangiqsualujjuaq continue to celebrate New Year's with a worship service, traditional games, and dancing. However, these festivities are no longer held in the school gym; they are now held in Kangiqsualujjuaq's other new public building — a sophisticated and spacious community centre built with provincial and federal government assistance.

The New Year's Eve that Shook Saint-Sauveur

In the 1940s, the sleepy Laurentian village of Saint-Sauveur was gaining a reputation as a prime destination for downhill skiing. Hundreds of young men and women from Montreal rode up on the Canadian National and Canadian Pacific "ski trains" to try out their planks on the downhill slopes. It was an exciting way to escape Montreal during the long winter months. Debonair young men and comely girls wearing knickers and bright patterned sweaters had lots of fun on the trains, playing card games, reading, and flirting. The train cars were packed with skis and ski poles that poked out like saplings from between the short bench seats.

Naturally, the skiers frequented local restaurants and hotels for some *après-ski* fun, but for the most part the skiers and the townspeople of Saint-Sauveur were like ships passing in the night, each group minding their own business. Or at least that was the case until one wild New Year's Eve in 1948. "There had never been something like that before and never again, either!" remembered André Joncas, a native of Saint-Sauveur.

On the afternoon of December 31, the train platform at Saint-Sauveur was buzzing with skiers intent on having a good time. The young people headed straight for the hills to get in a few runs, then they looked around for some refreshments. There were many drinking establishments in Saint-Sauveur, but a hotel tavern nicknamed "the Pub" was the most popular one with the skiers.

The Pub was a vast drinking room downstairs from the hotel's few spartan lodgings. It was a rustic spot with long wooden tables and benches like those in European drinking halls. There was no décor to speak of, but the people who congregated there didn't seem to mind — they were there for the beer.

"It was New Year's Eve and the beer was flowing. The lads began buying each other round upon round," recalled Joncas.

Around 10 p.m., the drinking reached a fever pitch. Suddenly, one of the skiers made an inappropriate comment to another skier, which led to a hard punch in the face. As the rascal fell to the ground, his friends rallied round to take revenge. More fistfights started to break out around the room, and several patrons ended up on the floor with bloody noses and bruised egos. When a row of beer bottles went careening off the end of a table and crashed onto the wooden floor, the brawl was in full swing.

By this point, the manager of the pub was fuming; he called in the local police. Now this was the 1940s, so the policemen had no reservations about marching in and hitting the drinkers with their *garcettes* (small leather sacks filled with sand) to stop them from punching each other. Then the police chief called in reinforcements from local families, including the St. Denis, Lamoureux, Trottier, and Flynn families.

The local police were busy pushing some of the rowdy kids down the stairs of the side entrance to the pub when two provincial police officers (who were called in by the overwhelmed Saint-Sauveur police) arrived in riding outfits.

The shorter of the two provincial constables jumped up on one of the tables, ordered the revellers to be quiet, and threatened that he and his partner would be back to check on things around midnight. But the police were in over their heads. There were just too many drunkards out of control. There was no anti-riot squad in 1949, so the policemen did not have many resources at their command. One of the provincial constables was later found doubled over because he had been knocked out by one of the revellers on the Rue Principale.

André Joncas witnessed this disgraceful situation. Though he was shocked, he was also intrigued because he was an amateur photographer. Looking for some dramatic shots, Joncas decided to go to the police station to see who was there.

"The police station was really just a room with a desk and two cells. There were hardly ever any prisoners, so one of the cells was used as sleeping quarters for the policeman on night duty and the other cell was usually unoccupied," said Joncas.

But in the first hours of New Year's Day 1949, the simple police station was in an uproar. M. Chartier, an inexperienced officer who had been hired for that night only, had the radio blaring and he had put about 15 people into one of the cells.

"It was just wild. They were all still hitting each other and yelling. The cell was so crowded that they could barely stand up," recalled Joncas.

Then around 3 a.m., hundreds of young people who had not been locked up formed an impressive crowd and paraded down Lafleur Street towards the police station. The crowd marched boldly down the street before the break of dawn, loudly demanding their friends' release.

Finally, around 5 a.m., the jailed skiers were released; they had sobered up and there was really no reason to keep them in a cell. After all, the lads hadn't even broken anything.

Christmas in Quebec

As the sun rose on the New Year, the noisy city kids went back to their hotels to catch up on their sleep. And the townspeople of Saint-Sauveur breathed a collective sigh of relief.

Chapter 7
Christmas Stories to Gladden the Heart

Christmastime is not a joyous event for all Quebecers. Some people are more melancholic than usual during the holidays because they feel like they are the only ones in the world who are not joining in the festivities. But then there are those Christmas angels, Quebecers who make an extra effort during this season to help both loved ones and complete strangers to enjoy a Christmas filled with love and caring.

Fleurette's Christmas Party
In November 1970, Fleurette Bilodeau went looking for elderly people in Longueuil, a Montreal suburb on the south shore of the St. Lawrence River. "I went through the streets in my car and when I saw houses that were in rough shape, I would

knock on the door. Then, when the occupant answered, I would pretend that I had the wrong address as an excuse, so that they would open the door. Of course, I did not want to say that I knocked on your door because your house is decrepit," she explained.

Fleurette's intentions were entirely honourable. She wanted to find elderly people who were poverty stricken or lonely, and then throw a Christmas party for them. By December 24, Fleurette had located 27 people — including a couple who had barely left the house in 11 years — and invited them all to her apartment for a traditional Christmas Eve celebration. There was a midnight mass, followed by a *réveillon* meal in the wee hours of the morning. Volunteers helped to make the turkey dinner and decorate the apartment, a Montreal religious order loaned the necessary dishes, and a child Fleurette knew provided the musical entertainment. Fleurette selected presents for each of the guests and financed the whole operation.

"I grew up in the Lac St. Jean region, one of 19 children, and as we were growing up we were taught to value older people," explained Fleurette.

Thirty-four years later, Fleurette Bilodeau, (now a senior citizen herself at 74 years old) is still organizing an annual Christmas party in Longueuil. The guest list has broadened somewhat to include other people in need, including disabled people, cancer patients, teenage mothers, and people in drug rehabilitation. However, the original mandate — to provide a Christmas celebration for people who would otherwise have a lonely time at Christmas — has not changed. Fleurette's first experience working with elderly people was in the late 1960s, when she joined the *Petits Frères des Pauvres*, a religious community in Montreal that she'd heard about from a family member. As a member of this community, she was fed, lodged, and paid five dollars a day in exchange for promises (not vows) that she would do her best to help underprivileged people. For two and a half years, Fleurette visited shut-ins and helped elderly people with domestic tasks. Then the philosophy of the *Petits Frères* changed in 1969 — members were given working hours (8 a.m. to 4 p.m.) and a salary, and they needed permission to leave the building. Fleurette resisted these restrictions.

"People can need you at any time, at eight o'clock at night or even at midnight. I could not stay there (at the *Petits Frères des Pauvres*) any more because it had changed too much," she said.

The next year, Bilodeau took a job in student services at Collège Marguerite-Bourgeoys in Westmount, and it was then that she organized her first Christmas party. By the time of the second Christmas party, in 1971, the guest list had more than doubled as information about the party spread throughout the community. Elderly people started calling Fleurette to ask if they could attend.

Meanwhile, Fleurette continued to seek out elderly people who were alone in the world. One such case was

Eugénie Vallée, a woman in her 60s who was bedridden due to a severe case of arthritis. Mme Vallée was barely able to walk, let alone take care of herself.

Fleurette began to visit Eugénie on a regular basis, and she added Eugénie's name to the growing list of Christmas party guests. Eugénie attended every Christmas celebration until she died. Every year, two students from College Marguerite-Bourgeoys would bathe her, dress her, and bring her to the party.

Fleurette realized early on that there was a ready-made team of volunteers at the college. Dozens of Marguerite-Bourgeoys students threw themselves into Fleurette's project with gusto. Not only did the students organize fundraising activities at the college, they also volunteered to perform a multitude of tasks, including helping to buy presents, wrapping presents, driving the guests to the party, decorating the hall, assisting with the entertainment, setting the tables, decorating the Christmas tree, greeting the guests, buying groceries, preparing the traditional turkey dinner, serving the dinner, singing in the improvised midnight mass choir, and helping to clean up at the end of the party.

Jean-Pierre Lapointe was a student volunteer more than 25 years ago. "I first helped out with the Christmas party when I was 17 years old," recalled Lapointe. "I wanted to do it because it felt good to deliver a service to the community and to help people during a period when it is very hard to be alone ... I wanted to find the real meaning of Christmas."

The first year that Jean-Pierre was involved, his mother was very proud that her son was going off to do volunteer work, and the Lapointe family simply celebrated Christmas the following day. But the second year, his parents decided that if Jean-Pierre was really moved by Fleurette's Christmas celebration, then the whole family ought to join him. So Jean-Pierre's parents, sister, and brother all volunteered to help.

"It became a family tradition," remarked Jean-Pierre.

Jean-Pierre and fellow volunteers got to know many of the Christmas party guests during the course of the year as they visited elderly people and brought hot meals. Some of the shut-ins whom the volunteers called on had not received visitors for weeks or even months.

In the months leading up to Christmas, Jean-Pierre and a dozen other students would begin to prepare for the Christmas party. Jean-Pierre became a proficient multi-tasker. "I approached businesses for donations, picked up food, wrapped presents, peeled potatoes, and blew up balloons. By the time the Christmas party ended in the wee hours of the morning, I had been standing up for about 30 hours in a row."

Jean-Pierre has not missed a Christmas party in 25 years. These days, he attends the parties with his wife and his teenage children. "I also think that it is important for my children to see something other than the happiness which they see at home. They are lucky to have parents who are in good shape and to not lack for anything, but they must also see that there are other things in the world, too. They are always happy to come help out," he said.

Jean-Pierre was one of 150 volunteers who helped to organize the 2003 Christmas party, which was held in the basement of the Saint-Charles-Borromée church in Longueuil. There were 400 guests at the event and Fleurette was quick to point out that during the week before the party, her volunteers also made 527 visits to people who were invited to the party but who were unable to come.

The Christmas party has been celebrated at lunchtime since 1996, because some of the elderly people were finding it too difficult to stay up late for the traditional midnight mass and *réveillon*. Yet the mass still begins with *"Minuit, Chrétiens!"* and the worship still follows the order of service of a traditional midnight mass.

Another aspect of the celebration that has changed over the years is that volunteers are no longer expected to sing in an improvised midnight mass choir. These days, Fleurette hires a professional musician who plays an electronic piano and sings the special Christmas hymns and carols.

At a recent Christmas party, Fleurette's guests were treated to a delicious *réveillon* meal with turkey, *tourtière*, cranberry sauce, mashed potatoes, cooked vegetables, and dessert. Then the singers who performed during the mass became the afternoon's entertainment. One of the musicians brought out a saxophone, another became the master of ceremonies, and the guests settled into the party atmosphere.

Volunteers who had sat with the guests while they finished up their dinner joined them for some old-fashioned dancing. Finally, the Christmas presents were distributed. Fleurette keeps a file for each guest with their age, sex, clothing size, and a record of past gifts. Every year, her guests receive two presents — one practical and one for pleasure. Presents for male guests typically include shirts, pyjamas, knitted socks, shaving lotion, or a deck of cards.

"It's more difficult to choose presents for women, because their dress size can change a lot. We start to buy the presents in September, so it is not possible to return anything," said Fleurette. Female guests generally receive slippers, scarves, household items like tablecloths and dish-towels, as well as some kind of beauty care product.

Remarkably, every year, Fleurette has been able to raise sufficient funds to cover all of her costs. In the fall, she sends out letters to friends and family in the Lac St. Jean region. Monies received from them, as well as the Club Optimiste in Longueuil, Club Richelieu de St. Lambert, and donations from old students cover the costs of hall rental, food, entertainment, and the Christmas presents.

Agathe Landry-Bouchard has been invited to the Christmas parties for 26 years in a row. Though Agathe has enough to eat and is not in a desperate situation, she is alone because she has no children and few friends.

"The beauty of Fleurette's event is that she does not exclude anyone. Some people come with beautiful jewellery and others practically have rags on their backs. The main criterion for Fleurette is loneliness. She does not want people to feel lonely at Christmas," explained Jean-Pierre Lapointe.

For more than 30 years, Fleurette Bilodeau has helped thousands of people to enjoy the religious and secular aspects of a traditional Christmas party. If not for Fleurette's concern, most of these people would have spent Christmastime in misery.

Christmas Greetings For Nancy B.

Christmas 1991 in Quebec City: the city was bright with multi-coloured lights strung up on evergreen trees, street musicians were performing well-known Christmas tunes, and people were scurrying about through snow-covered streets attending Christmas parties and buying gifts. But for 24-year-old Nancy Bolduc, Christmas of 1991 would not include parties or Christmas trees. Nancy was lying in bed at the Hôtel-Dieu Hospital, paralysed from the neck down ever since a rare viral disease called Guillain-Barré had attacked her nervous system. She had been looking at the same four walls for more than two years. Television was her main diversion.

At the beginning of December, Nancy's lawyer, Anne Lapointe, had gone to court to try to force Hôtel-Dieu to comply with Nancy's ardent desire to have her respirator unplugged. Justice Jacques Dufour said that he would not make a decision until after the Christmas holidays, because he knew that Nancy did not want her family to grieve for her during the holiday season.

Naturally, Quebec City was abuzz with Nancy's story. All of the local newspapers, radio, and television stations were following the story and delving into philosophical debates about quality of life.

For most Quebecers, Christmas is a time of joy and a celebration of life. So it seemed cruelly ironic that Nancy Bolduc's struggle to end her life was being debated during the festive season. Instead of writing Christmas cards and planning Christmas parties, many Quebec City families were caught up in heated arguments about assisted suicide.

One day, CJRP, a now-defunct AM radio station, received a call from someone who thought that perhaps the hosts, Simon Bédard and Jean-François Bertrand, could collect Christmas cards for Nancy. Nothing could be done to improve Nancy's condition, but the caller thought it would be a kind gesture for people to let Nancy know she was in their thoughts and prayers.

The hosts offered to collect the cards for Nancy and the very next day the cards started to arrive. There were all sorts of Christmas cards: short notes and rambling prose; home-made whimsical cards and conventional Christmas greetings; heart-felt wishes from small children and thoughtful messages from adults. Most of the greetings were in French, but there were also many cards in other languages, including English, Spanish and Italian.

When Anne Lapointe went to pick up the Christmas greetings collected by CJRP, she was handed a box brimming over with more than 1000 cards. Lapointe brought the box of Christmas cards to Nancy's bedside in a room in the intensive care section.

After Lapointe brought the box from the radio station, Nancy looked at the cards with her parents, her sisters, and her brother, who all visited the hospital regularly. Although Nancy needed someone to hold each card, she was able to read the messages for herself.

The cards did not make reference to Nancy's legal battle to end her life. They were pure and spontaneous Christmas greetings to provide comfort to Nancy and her family.

One Last Christmas Wish
In Christmas 2003, the Tremblay family learned first-hand about the power of love. The patriarch of the family, Édouard, was extremely ill, so his children Suzanne, Josée, and Marc — along with their spouses and children — joined their mother, Mathilde, at the family home in Chicoutimi.

Édouard had been diagnosed with lung cancer more than a year before, and the Tremblay family were reluctant witnesses to his slow and painful deterioration. He was clearly having more and more trouble breathing, and he was so weak that he had a difficult time walking across the room. Yet, somehow, Édouard mustered enough strength to celebrate one last Christmas with his family.

The holiday passed slowly, with Édouard spending most of his time sitting in his armchair in the living room. He watched his children and grandchildren passing through on their way to and from tobogganing and skating expeditions. From time to time, Mathilde would bring him a cup of tea and one of her famous Christmas cookies, and his children would poke in their heads to tell him their latest news and ask whether he needed anything. And that was just about right for Édouard. He was included in the family bustle, yet he wasn't required to spend a long time talking.

Sometimes Édouard would sit back in his armchair and close his eyes, exhausted by his efforts to breathe. He appeared to be in a deep, deep sleep. But when the grand-children chased each other around the house, yelling and squealing, a broad smile of joy flashed across his face.

On Christmas night, Édouard pulled himself into the kitchen to help peel potatoes for dinner. He diligently pre-pared each potato, as he had done for decades of family gatherings. Unfortunately, when everyone sat down to din-ner, Édouard was too ill to join them.

One afternoon, Édouard asked his six-year-old grand-daughter, Sara, what she was learning at her new school. She mentioned a Christmas song called *Petit Papa Noël*, but when prompted by Édouard to sing the traditional children's song about Santa Claus, Sara feigned shyness. So Édouard began, "*Petit papa noël, quand tu descendras du ciel...*" and then he paused as if he could not remember the words. Sara joined in with the next line, and then grandfather and granddaughter sang the rest of the song as a duet. Édouard was so entranced that he almost seemed to be reliving his own childhood.

The next day, Édouard's brother René was invited for lunch. Édouard proudly dressed for the occasion, discarding his faded housecoat and putting on a crisp striped shirt, black pants, and an elegant velour vest. He was in an uncharacteristically jocular mood, reminiscing with his brother and gently teasing Mathilde for not having lunch ready on time.

On December 28, Édouard's children and grandchildren began to leave Chicoutimi and go back to their respective homes. Christmas was over. That afternoon, Édouard suffered a respiratory attack, which led to his death two days later.

The Tremblay family was in shock as they turned their focus from celebrating Christmas to planning a funeral. However, beneath the despair and the grief, there was a real sense of gratitude that the family had had one last Christmas season with Édouard — somehow, he had postponed his death until after Christmas.

Doctors and nurses who work in palliative care settings are quite familiar with the concept of death postponement. According to Dr. Balfour Mount, co-founder of Montreal Royal Victoria Hospital's palliative care centre: "Some people appear to be able to wait until after a special occasion. We have had many cases of people who were extremely ill who seemed to hold on in order to see someone or to be part of a special event and then they died after that event had happened."

Édouard must have had a very strong desire to celebrate one last Christmas with his children and grandchildren. His love for his family and his ardent desire to share Christmas with them may have even enabled him to delay natural physical processes. Édouard's death immediately following Christmas supports the conclusions of research conducted by Dr. David P. Phillips, a sociologist with the University of California at San Diego.

Dr. Phillips has been studying the relationship between death rates and important social occasions in California for more than a decade. According to his research reports, the imminence of a social occasion to which a dying patient has strong emotional ties can affect the patient's date of death.

In one study, Dr. Phillips examined the death records of Chinese Californians over a 25-year period and discovered that there was a lower-than-average number of deaths among Chinese-Californians right before the Harvest Moon Festival, and a higher-than-average number of deaths immediately following the holiday. Dr. Phillips has also observed a similar mortality pattern among Jewish men immediately before and after Passover.

Édouard was mourned for the rest of the holiday season. Naturally, the months following his death were extremely difficult for family members — but his family never forgot how fortunate they were to have had one last Christmas with him.

Christmas in Quebec

Although the religious aspect of Christmas is of decreasing significance for many modern Quebecers, this holiday remains an extremely important time for everyone to visit with friends and family. In fact, spending *Les Fêtes* with loved ones is so meaningful that Quebecers are willing to travel great distances, overcome logistical hurdles, and, if need be, even postpone their own deaths in order to achieve that goal.

Select Bibliography

Aubry, Claude. *The Magic Fiddler and Other Legends of French Canada*. Toronto: Peter Martin Associates Ltd., 1968.

Berthiaume, André. *Jacques Cartier: l'Inaccessible Royaume*. Montréal: XYZ, 1996.

Brisson, Marcelle and Côté-Gauthier, Suzanne. *Montréal de vive mémoire 1900-1939*. Montréal: Triptyque, 1994.

Cartier, Jacques. *Voyages au Canada; Jacques Cartier Suivis du Voyage de Roberval*. Montréal: Comeau & Nadeau, 2000.

Choquette, Dr. Ernest. *Carabinades*. Montreal: Déom Frères, 1900.

Collard, Edgar Andrew. *Canadian Yesterdays*. Toronto: Longmans, Green & Co., 1955.

DeBilly, Pierre. "Une drôle de nuit de Noël." Châtelaine, December 1997.

Desautels, Yvon. *Les Coutumes de Nos Ancêtres*. Montréal: Éditions Paulines, 1984.

Hémon, Louis. *Maria Chapdelaine*. Montréal: Lefebvre, 1916.

Lamothe, Jacques. *Le Folklore du Temps des Fêtes*. Montréal: Guérin, 1982.

Lemay, L.P. *Fêtes et Corvées*. Lévis: Pierre-Georges Roy, 1898.

Massicotte, E-Z. *Conteurs Canadiens-Français du XIX siècle*. Montréal: C.O. Beauchemin & Fils, 1902.

Pelchat, André. "O! Tannenbaum: a sentimental homecoming brings Canada its first Christmas tree." *The Beaver*, December 2002/January 2003.

Phillips, David P. "Death takes a holiday: Mortality surrounding major social occasions." *The Lancet*. September 24, 1988.

Provencher, Jean. *Les Quatres Saisons dans la Vallée du Saint-Laurent*. Montréal: Éditions Boréal, 1988.

Ruel, Sylvie. "Une crèche pour Saint-Jean-Port-Joli." *Sélection Reader's Digest*, December 1988.

Talbot, Edward Allen. *Five Year's Residence in the Canadas*. London: Longman, 1824.

Select Bibliography

Tasso, Lily. "Le Noël des vieux amis de Fleurette." *Sélection Reader's Digest.* December 1985.

Tharp, Louise Hall. *The Baroness and the General.* Toronto: Little Brown & Co., 1962.

Vachon, Georgette. *Images de Roméo Vachon.* La Société Historique de Saguenay, Numéro 35, 1975.

Vanasse, Nancy. "Les Dessous d'Opération Nez Rouge." *Coup de Pouce,* December 1995.

Acknowledgements

The author gratefully acknowledges assistance from Pierre Vachon, Pierre Lambert, André Joncas, the Société d'histoire de la Rivière du Nord, the Société historique du Québec, and the Société historique de la Côte-Nord. I would also like to thank the librarians at the Salle Gagnon of the Bibliothèque Centrale de Montréal for their diligence and their interest in this project.

Photo Credits

About the Author

Megan Durnford is a freelance writer based in Montreal. Her articles have been published in magazines and newspapers across the country. For more than a decade, Megan has also worked on multimedia projects about scientific and historical topics.

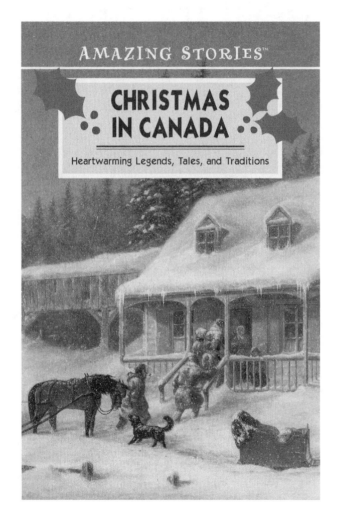

ISBN 1-55153-786-9

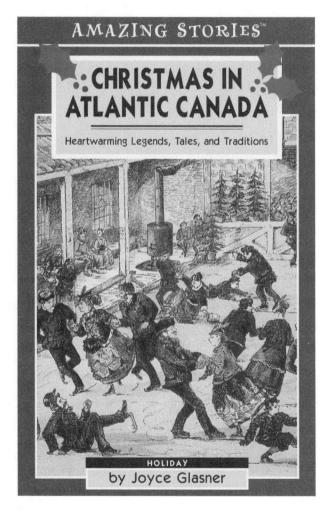

AMAZING STORIES™

.:CHRISTMAS IN :.
ATLANTIC CANADA

Heartwarming Legends, Tales, and Traditions

HOLIDAY
by Joyce Glasner

ISBN 1-55153-781-8

also available!

AMAZING STORIES™

CHRISTMAS IN ONTARIO

Heartwarming Legends, Tales, and Traditions

HOLIDAY

by Cheryl MacDonald

ISBN 1-55153-779-6

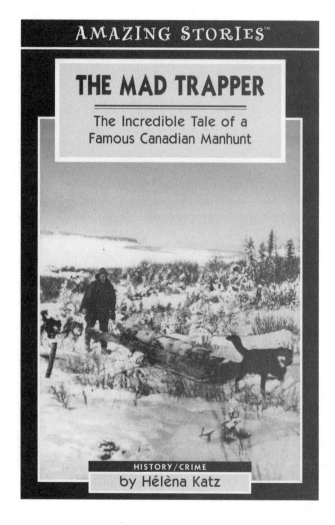

AMAZING STORIES™

THE MAD TRAPPER

The Incredible Tale of a
Famous Canadian Manhunt

HISTORY/CRIME
by Hélèna Katz

ISBN 1-55153-787-7